The Complete Guide To Dog Training

A How-To Set of Techniques and Exercises for Dogs of Any Species and Ages

© Copyright 2019 - All rights reserved.

The content contained within this book may not be reproduced, duplicated, or transmitted without direct written permission from the author or the publisher.

Under no circumstances will any blame or legal responsibility be held against the publisher or author for any damages, reparation, or monetary loss due to the information contained within this book, either directly or indirectly.

Legal Notice:

This book is copyright protected. It is only for personal use. You cannot amend, distribute, sell, use, quote, or paraphrase any part or the content within this book, without the consent of the author or publisher.

Disclaimer Notice:

Please note the information contained within this document is for educational and entertainment purposes only. All effort has been executed to present accurate, up to date, reliable, complete information. No warranties of any kind are declared or implied. Readers acknowledge that the author is not engaging in the rendering of legal, financial, medical, or professional advice. The content within this book has been derived from various sources. Please consult a licensed professional before attempting any techniques outlined in this book.

By reading this document, the reader agrees that under no circumstances is the author responsible for any losses, direct or indirect, that are incurred as a result of the use of information contained within this document, including, but not limited to, errors, omissions, or inaccuracies.

Table of Contents

Introduction: Training Your Dog 9

Chapter 1: Why Should You Train Your Dog? 11

    Important Reasons Why Dog Training is Essential 12

    What Happens When You Don't Train Your Dog? 16

    FAQs About Dog Training 19

    Dog Training Mistakes to Avoid 24

Chapter 2: Dog Training Basics 29

    Different Methods of Dog Training 30

    Tips for Getting Started 35

    Things You Need for Dog Training 39

    Basic Commands and How to Teach Them 43

Chapter 3: Training Puppies 50

    How Early Should You Start? 52

    Coming Up with a Training Schedule for Your Puppy 54

        When your puppy is 8 weeks old 54

        When your puppy is 9 weeks old 58

        When your puppy is 10 weeks old 59

        When your puppy is 12 weeks old 60

        When your puppy is 16 weeks old 60

    Potty-Training Your Puppy 61

    Practical Tips for Training Puppies 65

Chapter 4: Training Young Dogs 72

    Learning from Older Dogs 73

Top Tips for Training Young Dogs 74

Chapter 5: Training Adult Dogs 80

House-Training Adult Dogs 85

Basic Obedience Training for Adult Dogs 87

Adult Dog Training Tips from Experts 89

Training Adult Dogs to Do New Tricks 91

Chapter 6: Training Senior Dogs 92

Things to Remember When Training Senior Dogs 95

Helpful Tips for Training Senior Dogs 99

Chapter 7: Training Different Dog Breeds 103

Dog Breeds and Behaviors 103

The Easiest Dog Breeds to Train 106

The Most Challenging Dog Breeds to Train 110

General Tips for Training Different Dog Breeds 114

Chapter 8: Common Behavioral Issues in Dogs and How to Deal with Them 119

Training Hyperactive Dogs to Calm Down 119

Play Biting, Mouthing, and Nipping 122

Chewing, Digging, and Other Destructive Behaviors . 126

Barking, Whining, and Other Noisy Behaviors 128

Chapter 9: Rewards and Punishments 131

Reward-Based Training 133

Positive Reinforcement Training 135

Should Punishments Be Part of Your Training? 138

Effective Ways to Discipline Your Dog 140

Chapter 10: Advanced Training Tips and Tricks 144

Precision Dog Training 145

Tips for Training Working Dogs 147

Training Small Dogs 149
Training Large Dogs 150
More Advanced Training Tips and Tricks 152
Conclusion: Training Your Dog the Right Way *154*
References *156*

Introduction: Training Your Dog

Fig. 1: Trained Dog. From Unsplash, by Reed

Whether you are a new dog owner or are just thinking about bringing a furry friend into your home, you should know that training your dog is an essential part of the process. Dog training is more than simply teaching your dog commands and tricks. It involves intentional communication with your canine companion. Training your dog requires a lot of practice, which means that you will have to communicate continuously for life! Although socialization with other dogs helps with domestication, your dog should also learn how to properly communicate with people. The most effective way to do this is through training—a clear and consistent form of canine education with a foundation of mutual respect and trust.

There are different ways to train dogs, and it's up to you to find the most effective method for you and for your furry friend. To do this, you should try to achieve a balance between yourself and your dog in their life and in their environment. To achieve balance, you should learn how to communicate effectively with your dog; create structure in your dog's environment and in your relationship with them, improve the relationship you have established, and reduce the natural latent stress that dogs experience in their lives.

In doing all of this as part of your training, your pet will start paying more attention to you. In fact, your dog may even start looking forward to obeying you or following your lead. Training your dog won't be a short or easy process. You must invest a lot of time and money into it. Of course, this doesn't mean that you can't have fun along the way too! In this book, you will learn everything you need to know about training your dog. From the basics to more advanced tips and everything in between, our discussions will help make dog training much easier for you. Whether you have a puppy, a young dog, an adult dog, or even an older one, we've got you covered.

The more time you spend training your canine companion, the more you will see your bond strengthen. Focusing intently on your dog while training makes your dog trust you more profoundly. Over time, you may even learn how to anticipate your dog's behavior, thus making it easier for you to train them. Furthermore, having a well-trained dog means that you can allow them to explore the world freely without having to worry about their safety—or the safety of the people around them!

Chapter 1: Why Should You Train Your Dog?

Dog training is an important aspect of a dog's life, and as a pet owner, it's your responsibility to ensure that it is done properly. Training provides your dog with mental and physical stimulation to keep them happy, healthy, and well-rounded. Positive training techniques are enjoyable for dogs, and they help strengthen your relationship. For such techniques, you will set-up your dog to succeed, then reward them for their good behaviors. The rewards you give your canine while training may come in the form of treats, verbal praise, or even physical affection. Each time your dog does something good, especially after you have taught the action, you can give the reward.

In general, many dog trainers who use these kinds of training methods also ignore "bad" behaviors. That way, your dog won't be rewarded in any kind of way—sometimes, paying attention based on bad behaviors seems like a "reward," which is why ignoring them is much more effective. Therefore, if your dog doesn't receive a reward for doing something (because it's bad) and they don't receive attention either, the chances are that they will stop doing the behavior. For instance, if you have an overly excited dog who loves jumping up when you get home, you can ignore your dog throughout this specific behavior. Once your dog gets back down on the floor, that's when you look at them and give them positive attention. In instances where you come home, and they greet you without jumping, then you can reward them for this.

One thing you must avoid when training your dog is using physical punishment. Contrary to some beliefs, hitting your dog doesn't actually stop bad behaviors. Most of the time, physical punishments will even make matters worse!

Seeing as dog training is the responsibility of owners, learning everything you can about how to train your dog is crucial. And the earlier you start, the more beneficial for yourself and your dog.

Important Reasons Why Dog Training is Essential

Through the years, dogs have become known as man's best friend, and the main reason for this is that they are social and pack animals. Dogs kept as pets look to their owners to guide them so that they can learn how to behave as expected. Unless you teach the rules to your dog, don't expect them to know what your rules are. Dog training is essential as it provides your canine with the education they need to be a well-behaved, functional member of your family. Here are some of the most important benefits of dog training:

- **Your dog will learn how to listen to you**

    While your dog may listen to you when you call their name, this doesn't mean that they will follow your orders. But through training, you'll discover that your dog is listening to you—really listening. Although they won't listen every time you say something, your dog will learn what the commands you say really mean. Then, they will start following you more frequently than before.

- **You will be able to control your dog more easily**

    Later on, you will learn about the basic commands to teach your dog—and how to teach them. Training your dog to learn these basic commands will help you control your dog easily and more effectively, no matter what the situation is. Whether you are at home or decide to take your dog out for a walk, these commands will also keep your canine companion safe.

- **Dog training can save your dog's life**

    When dogs get scared, they tend to run away, and this can be extremely dangerous for them, especially if they run into the streets. But when you have trained your dog to come back when you call their name, this can save their life.

- **It gives you a lot of opportunities to have fun with your dog**

    While you are training or during breaks, you can have a lot of fun with your dog. For training, you can find fun ways to teach your dog basic (or even advanced) tips and tricks. During breaks, you can play with your dog. No matter what species you belong to, play is always a lot of fun!

- **Dog training provides your dog with a solid foundation**

    Teaching the basic commands to your canine provides them with a solid foundation to help you deal with different kinds of circumstances and situations. Then, as you teach your dog new tricks, you can incorporate the basics to reinforce them and strengthen your dog's learning process. Again, the longer you stick with your dog training, the more you will see improvements in how they behave and react in various situations.

- **It gives you a better understanding of your dog**

    Training your dog involves spending a lot of quality time with your them. Because of this, you will be able to gain a better understanding of your canine's unique signals and body language. And when you understand your dog better, you will be able to train them better too.

- **It strengthens your bond**

    From the get-go, you should be able to establish a strong connection with your dog; otherwise, they won't listen to you. After establishing that strong connection, training your dog using the proper techniques and methods will help make your bond even stronger. The great news is that once you have trained your dog well, you will notice that they are more confident, relaxed, manageable, and content. Your dog will also trust you more, thus making them happier and more willing to listen.

- **Training your dog with other dogs teaches valuable socialization skills**

    You don't have to train your dog alone. Once in a while, you can bring your dog to the park and join other pet owners who are training their dogs too. You also have the option to enroll your pet in obedience classes to learn with other dogs. Either way, when your dog is trained with other dogs, they learn how to socialize with each other—another essential skill for a well-rounded canine.

- **Dog training provides the stimulation needed to stay happy and healthy**

    Training provides your canine with many different types of stimulation. These include physical exercise, mental stimulation, quality time with you, and you may even teach them responsibility. Apart from these, your dog will also enjoy all of the rewards they get each time they do something right.

As you can see, dog training is beneficial for you and for your dog as well. With all of these benefits and more, you should see why it's important to train your dog as soon as possible. You can start enjoying all of these benefits while helping your dog grow into a well-rounded, well-mannered, and happy adult dog.

What Happens When You Don't Train Your Dog?

Fig. 2: Growling Dog. From Pixabay, by Rain

No matter how much you love your dog, there will be things they do that you will not approve of, and if you want things to change, training is key. An untrained dog may think that they are in charge at home, and they might end up driving you crazy! They bark incessantly, chew up all of your shoes, and run after your visitors nipping at their heels. If you're unwilling to train your dog, you might just throw them a toy or some other objects just to get them to stop.

Does this situation sound familiar to you?

Well, if you continue doing this instead of putting in the effort to train your dog, don't expect things to improve. When dogs act inappropriately or do "bad" things, the problem doesn't lie with them; it lies with you, their owner. For untrained dogs, they do these things because it's part of their nature. Unless you teach your dog the "right" things, the behaviors you dislike will continue. And this might make living with your dog extremely challenging.

Just as you wanted to make your dog a member of your family, your dog wants you to step up and lead. The truth is that dogs have an innate need for security and social structure. Unless you take the role of the leader, your dog will feel like they are in charge, and this is when the bad behaviors may start. Here are some things that may happen when you don't train your dog:

- **Your dog gets bored**

    Bored dogs engage in activities such as barking, digging, chewing, pacing, and jumping on you. This is why one of the most important benefits of dog training is stimulation. Dogs need to be stimulated so that they won't act out. A bored dog has nothing better to do, so they will simply do whatever they feel like!

- **Your small dog will develop "small dog syndrome"**

    Small dogs don't know that they are small. Just because you have an adorable toy dog, that doesn't mean you don't have to train them. Without the proper training, your canine companion might turn into a nasty, short-tempered terror!

- **Your big dog will become a wrecking ball**

    While small dogs may become prima donnas, big dogs who haven't been trained can start destroying everything around them! If you have a big dog at home, don't let their size intimidate you. Training is still important no matter how big your dog is, especially if you want to keep your home and belongings intact.

- **Your dog will start landscaping your yard**

    All dogs love to dig as part of their exploration. They dig to investigate things they smell, they dig when searching for food, and they may even dig to escape your backyard. Digging is a destructive and dangerous behavior that won't go away unless you train your dog that this isn't okay.

- **Your dog will chew everything in sight**

    Dogs love chewing things, especially while they are puppies. They don't do this to annoy you; they just like to chew! Unfortunately, unless you give your dog a chew toy or you train your dog not to chew your things, you might come home to see your pillows, the legs of your chairs, and the cords of your electronic appliances all chewed up!

- **Your dog will keep you up all night by howling and barking**

    It's good if your dog barks or howls when they spot an intruder in the vicinity. But when they do it all day and all night, it will surely drive you mad. The good news is that you can actually teach your dog to bark only when appropriate. How do you do this? Through dog training, of course!

- **Your dog will have accidents all around your house**

    Although you may have already housebroken your dog, don't think that this is all the training they need. Otherwise, you might notice that your canine companion is leaving you surprises all around your house. House-training is one of the most basic—and most important—things to train your dog. And you need to keep practicing this so that your dog doesn't forget. Also, you should continue training and stimulating your canine even after they have learned a lot of tricks, as this provides them with the stimulation they need.

- **Your dog becomes sad**

    Just like us, dogs can get the blues, especially when they experience a major loss or change in their lives. To perk up your dog, start a training schedule. This gives you time to communicate and interact with your dog, which are activities they really enjoy. If you notice that your dog is feeling sad, play with them, train them, and talk to them to lift their spirits. But if the blues go on for more than a few days or weeks, you should consider taking them to the vet.

As you can see, not training your dog can lead to many negative consequences. This is why dog training is considered the responsibility of the owners. Since dogs cannot train themselves, you have to step up to the challenge!

FAQs About Dog Training

Before you learn the basics of dog training, you may have some questions in your mind about the whole process. As previously mentioned, dog training is an essential part of a dog's life; therefore, as an owner, you must make this happen. When you bring a dog into your home and make that dog a part of your life, you must also teach them how to fit in. Dog training also helps you learn about your dog's needs and personality. The more you learn, the more you can make adjustments in your expectations to strengthen your bond and improve your relationship.

Take the time and put in the effort to train your dog to avoid frustrations and ensure a happy life with your canine companion. To help you understand dog training even further, let's answer some of the most common questions people ask about it.

1. **What's the best method for training dogs?**

   While there are many methods you can choose from when it comes to dog training, make sure to focus on those that are dog-friendly. This type of training is all about learning how to understand your dog and meet all of their needs. Remember that dogs are individuals, just like us. This means that although there are general methods for training, you must make sure that you customize your methods to make them kind, gentle, effective, and humane. Dog-friendly training methods encourage positive behaviors while ignoring the negative ones. These methods don't incorporate coercion, intimidation, or physical punishment that causes emotional, mental, or physical pain to your furry friend. Even if you think that your dog has "behavioral problems," it's never a good idea to use such methods, as these can make the situation worse. Beyond this, it is up to you as an owner to determine the best method for training your own dog. You may have to do some experimentation to see what works and what doesn't.

2. How to train dogs in a dog-friendly way?

The first thing you must do is to learn everything you need in terms of the methodology and principles of how to teach the behaviors you want your dog to have. Fortunately, you have purchased this book that contains a wealth of information to help you learn about dog-friendly training. You can also watch videos online or attend dog training classes to reinforce everything that you learn here.

3. How to stop your dog from jumping up at you each time you get home?

When your dog jumps up at you when you get home, this shows how excited they are that you have finally returned. Unfortunately, this isn't an ideal behavior. As part of your dog's training, you train your dog to jump on you only when you give a specific command. For instance, when you say something like "Play," then your dog can jump up. But once you give another command such as "Stop" or "Enough," your dog must stop. Practice these commands with your dog to make them stick.

4. How to stop your puppy from whining or crying at night?

This is an easy one. To stop the whining, crying or barking, you simply have to ignore it. Although this can be extremely challenging, it is the most effective thing to do. If you keep checking on your puppy throughout the night, shush them, or do anything else to acknowledge their whining, they will keep doing it. But when you ignore these behaviors, over time, your puppy will learn that whining, barking, or crying won't get them anywhere.

5. How to correct your puppy or young dog when they have a house-training accident?

The only time you should correct your puppy or young dog is when you catch them in the act. Young dogs learn by association. This means that when you see your young dog or puppy pooping or peeing where they shouldn't be, correct the behavior right away. When you see the "surprise" left by your young dog but they are nowhere in sight, there is no point in trying to correct them. While your puppy is performing the unwanted behavior, clap your hands while saying "NO!" in an urgent tone. Then carry your puppy to where they should be doing their business and give the proper command.

6. Why do some people opt for dog training classes?

Some people might not have the time, patience, or knowledge to train their dogs on their own. This is probably why they enroll their pets in dog training or obedience classes. While these programs are very effective, training your dog at home comes with more benefits. For one, you will be able to learn more about your dog. You will also have the chance to spend quality time with your dog each day, thus strengthening your bond. There is also the benefit of knowing exactly what your dog is capable of and what you need to improve on. Also, these dog training classes may cost a lot of money! One great benefit of these classes is that your dog will have a chance to socialize with other dogs while training. But you can have the same benefit when you train in the park or when you train with your friends who are training their dogs too.

7. Should you wait until your puppy has received all of the required vaccines before you start training?

This is a very common misconception that causes dog owners to delay their dog training. Yes, it's important to make sure that your puppy gets all the necessary vaccines. But you can start training your puppy even before the completion of these shots. Just make sure that you continue taking your puppy to the vet throughout your training until your little friend has received all the vaccinations they need.

8. What is clicker training?

This is a type of motivational, positive training method that has its basis in operant conditioning and the scientific principles of learning theory. The fundamental principle of this training method is that rewarding behaviors reinforce or "make stronger," therefore, encouraging the subject to do them more often. For clicker training, you would use a tiny mechanical clicker to indicate the precise moment when your dog is doing the behavior you requested. Then. you would immediately give a reward after the sound. The great news about clicker training is that it works effectively for all dog breeds!

Dog Training Mistakes to Avoid

Dog training doesn't just provide essential stimulation for your dog; it also teaches them how to behave well. But when it comes to training dogs, there are some mistakes dog owners make that may cause more harm than good. For one, over-training your canine is never a good idea. This might undo all of the training your dog has already learned along with the time and effort you have already invested. To give you a better idea of the mistakes to avoid, here are the most common ones:

Not considering your dog's age

While training your puppy while still young is a good thing—especially since early life experiences are crucial—you should never set intense and long training sessions for your puppy. When you start off with difficult training sessions or you try to teach too many things, this will have adverse consequences on your young dog. While they may obey you, they do so fearfully and grudgingly. Then, they grow up that way instead of being eager, enthusiastic, and happy about pleasing you.

Consider your training carefully if you have a senior dog too. While it's possible to train older dogs, they may suffer from medical conditions and muscle or joint soreness that might make learning difficult for them. Some senior dogs also experience a decrease in their cognitive abilities as they age. Therefore, when training a senior dog, you may need more patience and time before you will see results.

Not following the training schedule you set for your dog

In the beginning, you may feel very enthusiastic while training your dog. You set a schedule that includes short, frequent sessions and follow it religiously. Over time, you may get tired of your training sessions, especially when you see that your dog has already learned a few tricks. Because of this, you start missing your training sessions until you forget them altogether.

Unfortunately, when you don't train your dog frequently, this causes them to go on "auto-pilot." Over time, your dog might forget the things they've learned, and the behaviors you have worked to eliminate have come back. If you want your training to stick, and you want your dog to have the stimulation they need, make sure that you train regularly and consistently.

Repeating commands until your dog obeys

This is a very common mistake. You try to teach a command, such as "Stay," but your dog is distracted or confused, so they don't respond. So, you keep repeating the command until your dog performs the action halfheartedly. What your dog learns here is to keep stalling until you have repeated the command several times—and this learned behavior is very hard to unlearn.

Say a command once. If your dog ignores you, they might not have heard you, they may be distracted, you might not have taught it correctly, or your dog is simply rebelling against you. Bring your dog to a quieter environment and say the command again. If you are still ignored, re-teach the command until your dog learns how to do it again. But if your dog follows you, praise them!

Generalizing your training instead of customizing it for your own dog

Each dog has a unique behavioral profile and personality. Instead of generalizing your dog, try to understand them more before you proceed with your training. Experiment with different training methods until you determine which method is most effective with your canine companion. If you discover that some methods don't work, make the necessary adjustments. If you see that your dog enjoys a particular method of training, find ways to incorporate this method while teaching other behaviors, lessons, or tricks to your dog. Even though there are general or basic methods for training, learning which ones work for your dog is key to the success of your dog training.

Trying to do too many things, too fast

Have you ever felt overwhelmed at work when you were assigned too many different tasks to complete by the end of the day? Well, dogs can feel overwhelmed too! Some owners try to teach too many things at once or force their dogs to train for hours on end just to speed things along. However, this isn't good for your dog. In fact, when your dog gets overwhelmed,

Fig. 3: Overwhelmed. From Pixabay, by Ella_87, 2019, https://pixabay.com/photos/dog-cavalier-

they won't be able to learn anything. Try focusing on a maximum of two commands or tasks for each training session. Keep practicing until your dog has actually learned these commands before moving on to new ones. Remember, patience is key.

Giving too many treats and not giving praise

While dogs love treats, and giving them reinforces good behaviors, giving too many won't be good for your dog. This might cause a fixation on food instead of learning the behaviors themselves. Try to balance the rewards you give. Give your dog treats, praises, and affectionate gestures as needed. Try to determine which is appropriate to get the best response from your dog at each training session.

Not having enough confidence while training

When you're not confident enough, your dog will see this as a weakness. They sense this instinctively, and when your dog senses this lack of confidence in you, they might not listen to or follow you. Your dog might even exploit this weakness of yours because it is their nature. To increase your confidence, you may want to attend dog training classes, especially at the beginning of your training. When you feel more confident to train on your own, start at home. The more confidence you gain, the more you can try training your dog in different environments.

Being too emotional

Finally, when you show too much emotion while training, this tends to have an effect on your dog's learning ability. For instance, when you are angry, irritated, or forceful while training, you might intimidate your dog, making them fearfully obedient. Conversely, when you show too much energy, squeal with delight each time your dog does something right, or jump around as much as your dog, this will have an adverse effect on how they learn and focus. While training, it's best to show calm indifference. Have a demeanor that suggests easy authority and competence. This laid-back kind of energy where you show love and guidance calms your dog down and helps with your confidence too.

Chapter 2: Dog Training Basics

Once you bring a dog into your life, you won't be able to imagine your life without them. Dog owners adore and admire their canine companions for their enthusiasm, unconditional affection, and loyalty. But when man's best friend keeps chewing things up, barking all night, digging the yard, and so on, you might not appreciate them as much. If you want to make the most out of your bond with your canine, you must train them to help you live harmoniously. When you train your dog, it improves both your lives, and it also ensures both your safety. The great thing about dogs is that they love to learn—and you can teach them through good communication. You should help your dog understand how they should behave and why following you is in their best interest.

Any responsible dog owner should learn how to train their dog. Training is also a fun and enriching way to bond with your canine companion. Part of your dog's training is to set clear boundaries. While training your dog, make sure that you clearly define these boundaries so that your dog learns to respect them. To do this, you will have to train your dog to follow commands that are very specific. This makes it easier for you to enforce the boundaries you've set consistently. Just like any other skill, you must start with the basics when you're learning how to train your dog. The same thing goes for when you're actually training—start with the basics, practice, then move on when you think you (or your dog) are ready for the more advanced stuff. Looking at dog training as an adventure to take with your canine companion makes it more fun for both of you. And the more you learn before you start training, the more confident you will be throughout the process.

Different Methods of Dog Training

When it comes to dog training, there are many different methods you can choose from. But when you know nothing about these methods, how can you determine which one to use for your dog? Hearing about all of these methods might make you feel confused and overwhelmed. Don't worry, because all dog owners experience this, especially at the beginning of their dog-training journey. For you to choose the best method for training your dog, you'll first need to learn more about them. Here are the most common training methods for you to consider:

- **Alpha Dog Training (Dominance Training)**

  For this type of training, you would depend on the natural pack mentality of your dog. Since this is their instinct, you can use it to build a relationship of appropriate dominance and submission. This training method is based on the theory that dogs consider you and your whole family as a pack—their pack. Here, you must establish your role as the alpha in order for your dog to respect and obey you. If you plan to use this method, you will have to understand the body language of your dog and learn how to respond appropriately while projecting confidence and authority. Since there is a struggle of dominance here, you need to put emphasis on reinforcing your dog's training consistently.

- **Behavioral Training**

    This method of training refers to any kind of training method where dogs learn how to be well-behaved around people and around other animals. Behavioral training may include teaching basic commands too, but your main goal here is to teach your dog how to be a "good citizen." Some trainers use this method to reduce or eliminate behavioral issues. This is the most common and most basic training method for puppies and young dogs.

- **Positive Reinforcement Training**

    This training method was popularized by more modern dog trainers. It's a fairly straightforward practice for training dogs as it involves rewarding good behaviors. Here, you would encourage your dog to repeat good behaviors by immediately giving rewards after they are done. When your dog does something bad, you would either ignore the behavior or take away their rewards.

- **Obedience Training**

    This type of training method focuses on teaching your dog how to obey you by following the commands that you use. It's a bit more advanced than behavioral training, but it can help you deal with behavioral problems even before they begin. This is another training method that's ideal for young dogs.

- **Scientific Training**

    Coming up with a definition for this training method is quite challenging since it relies heavily on information that is constantly changing and building. Your aim here would be to understand the nature of your dog, their abilities, and how effective punishments and rewards would be when used. The information for this training method comes from animal experts and behaviorists who continuously create new experiments and studies to help us understand the psychology of our four-legged friends. Before you can correct your dog's behaviors, you must understand them first.

- **Agility Training**

This is the perfect training method to use if you plan to let your dog participate in different dog sports, such as jumping, racing, and maneuvering through obstacle courses. This training method is more advanced, so your dog should already know and understand the basics before you begin. During competitions, you won't be allowed to reward or touch your dog. This means that you should have a very strong bond with your dog so that they can complete the sports by taking cues from your physical gestures and verbal commands only.

- **Clicker Training**

This method of training has its basis on operant conditioning, much like positive reinforcement training. As a matter of fact, some trainers believe that this training method may be part of the positive reinforcement training method. The only difference is that you would use a small mechanical device that makes quick and sharp noises to signal to your dog that they have performed the behavior you have requested.

- **Vocational Training**

    Just like us, dogs have the capacity to learn different skills. Some dogs learn how to hunt, do rescue work, assist handicapped individuals, and more. If you want your dog to have such skills, you can use the vocational training method. For this method, you will teach your dog very specific commands and techniques to communicate with the people around them and enhance their senses. You should know, however, that vocational training is both time-consuming and rigorous.

- **House-Training (with or without Crate-Training)**

    This training method is essential, especially if you want your dog to live indoors. Basically, you would train your dog to "do their business" in the proper locations. This is one of the first methods of training you must do. While you can do house-training on its own, crate-training can make the process easier. This is where you would keep your dog contained (inside a crate) to strengthen your training and make it flow smoothly.

- **Model-Rival Training (Mirror Training)**

    This method of dog training relies on learning through observation. You can do this by allowing your puppy or young dog to observe an adult or older dog who has already been trained. This provides a good role model for your dog to mimic. If you don't have another dog, you can also ask one of your friends or family members to act as the role model and pretend as if you are training them. As your dog observes, they learn the correct behaviors from the model.

- **Leash Training**

    All dogs must learn how to walk on a leash—unless you plan to keep yours confined within your property, which, incidentally, isn't good for the dog. When you take your dog outside, you must use a leash to comply with the local laws in most areas and to keep your dog safe as well. This is another essential training method that teaches your dog the proper way to walk while on a leash. This makes walking a more enjoyable experience for yourself and your dog too.

- **Relationship-Based Training**

    This method of training is a combination of other training methods. For this, the focus is on an individualized approach for yourself and your dog. The driving force in this training method is the relationship that exists between you and your canine. Therefore, the stronger your relationship is, the more effective your training will be.

While there are other types of dog training methods out there, these are the most common—and the ones that don't use physical or harsh punishments. Now that you know the basic information about these methods, you can have a better idea of which training method you want to use or which one would be most suitable for yourself and your canine companion.

Tips for Getting Started

Fig. 4: Getting Started. From Unsplash, by Wyatt Ryan, 2017,

So, you finally take your dog home. After a few days, it's time to start your dog's training. Ideally, you would have already learned all that you can about dog training by attending dog training classes, watching dog training videos, and reading dog training literature while you were still thinking about bringing a dog home. Of course, if you're reading this book and your dog is already in your home, that's okay too. The important thing is to educate yourself first before you can start educating your furry friend.

If you bring home a puppy, you must understand that puppies aren't small adult dogs; they are infant dogs. Therefore, you shouldn't expect too much from your puppy. Instead, consider their mental and physical limitations. When it comes to choosing the name of your dog, do so wisely. Choose a respectable name that you won't feel ashamed of even when you're training your dog in public places. Also, choose a name that makes you feel good, not one that other people might laugh at.

As soon as you bring your puppy home, give them a bottle filled with warm water along with a ticking clock. Place these items in your puppy's sleeping area as they will imitate the heartbeat and heat of your puppy's littermates. This will help soothe your puppy, especially at the beginning. Even if you bring home a young, adult, or senior dog from the shelter, there are many things you can do to make your new dog comfortable in their new home. After this, it's time to start preparing for your dog training sessions. For this task, here are some pointers to start off with:

- **Prepare a pen, baby gates, or a crate for your puppy**

    Whenever you aren't around to supervise your puppy directly, you must place them in a safe place, such as a pen, a crate, or a room closed off with baby gates. Then, provide safe toys for your puppy to play with or chew on while you're not around. Make sure that the area you place your puppy in doesn't contain any dangerous items or objects that your puppy might end up destroying. This helps ensure that your puppy won't learn any bad habits early on.

    Also, think about giving your puppy their own room. This should be a place where your puppy can sleep and have "alone time," a place that isn't being used by any other person or pet. If your puppy stays in their "room" quietly, you can reward them for it. You can also use a crate as their room. Crates are also very helpful when it's time for you to start house-training.

- **Remember that dogs don't understand English—or any other language**

    Puppies aren't born with the innate ability to understand our language. So, when you bring your puppy home, don't expect them to understand you when you say "no." If you want your puppy to understand what this word means, demonstrate what you want them to do when you say "no." Also, dogs don't think like us humans. They don't do things to anger you, they don't make plans for revenge, and they don't hold grudges. They simply do what makes them feel safe or happy; this is their nature.

- **Provide your dog with enough mental and physical stimulation**

   When dogs feel bored, they tend to get into trouble—no matter what age they are. This is why it's important for you to provide enough stimulation. The best way to do this is through short but meaningful training sessions. In particular, mental and physical stimulation helps with the growth and development of puppies.

- **Try catching your dog doing good things**

   It's important to observe your dog as much as you can to get a better sense of their personality and behaviors. While it's a lot easier to catch dogs doing bad things than scolding them after, how often do you catch your dog doing something good? You should be able to catch these instances as well because this is the perfect time to show your dog that what they just did is the right thing.

   After seeing behavior that you approve of, it's time to reward your dog using positive reinforcement. This can come in the form of treats, toys, affection, praise, and other good things. Rewarding your dog sends them a message that they are doing the right things. Just make sure that the rewards you give come immediately after the good behavior. Otherwise, you might be rewarding a different behavior altogether.

- **Once in a while, use high-value treats while training**

    Dog treats will always make your dog happy. But once in a while, try giving your dog high-value, healthy treats like liver, cheese, or chicken breast. You might be surprised at how hard your dog will work to get such treats. While store-bought dog treats will be effective while training in environments free of distractions, when you plan to train in new environments, you may want to bring better treats to keep your dog engaged. Just make sure the treats are soft and easy to chew so that you don't have to take long pauses while training.

- **Set "dog time" for your training sessions when your sole focus will be on your dog**

    One of the best things about dogs is that they live in the moment. The most important thing to them is what is happening right now. A few minutes later, that important moment is already forgotten. This is why you should focus on your dog during your training sessions. Think of this as "dog time," when you shouldn't be doing or thinking about anything else.

- **Always end your training sessions positively**

    This is an excellent way to keep your dog excited about your training sessions. Throughout the training session, your dog tried their best to impress you and make you happy. So, you should end your session with a few minutes of play, some petting, a treat, or plenty of praise.

- **Show happiness whenever your dog approaches you**

    Whether you are training, called your dog over, or didn't call your dog, when your dog comes to you, show them how happy you are. Call your dog's name in a playful and happy tone, and if they came to when you called, don't forget the reward!

Things You Need for Dog Training

After deciding what type of method to use and preparing your home, your dog, and yourself for training, it's time to gather all the basic tools you need for the task. The great thing about these basic tools is that you can use them throughout your training—from beginning to advanced training.

1. **Durable leash (at least 6-feet in length)**

    While you may have already bought a leash for your dog, you need one that's at least 6-feet long for training purposes. Also, choose one that allows you to get a solid grip on your furry friend. If you want a professional-grade leash, choose one that's made of sturdy leather, nylon, or cotton. Among all of these materials, leather is the most flexible and durable while being comfortable to hold too. Leather is also strong enough to withstand untrained dogs who tend to pull hard.

Helping your dog to develop a positive association with their leash makes it easier for you to get them into cars or go out for walks. You can help develop this positive association by feeding your dog training treats each time you clip it on.

2. Target stick

This tool is helpful when you need to teach both basic and complex tricks or behaviors. You can get a simple target stick or one with other features like a clicker that's already built-in or a target stick that collapses.

3. Collar (or harness)

For the purpose of positive reinforcement training or other training methods, you should consider choosing a simple collar with a flat-buckle and metal hardware. Metal buckles are more secure and durable than those made of plastic. If you have a dog with a narrow head—like a whippet or a greyhound—choose a martingale collar. You can tighten this collar enough to prevent your dog from slipping out of it but not so much that it ends up choking your dog. On the other hand, if you have a dog with a flat face—like a bulldog or a pug—you may want to opt for a harness instead of a collar.

4. Portable mat

Although some don't think it's essential, this tool will provide your pooch with a safe space to relax wherever you take them. Portable mats are easy to transport and wash. You may even choose one that has a sticky bottom to provide better stability.

5. Clicker

If you plan to use clicker training, you definitely need to get a clicker for yourself. Use this to indicate when your dog has performed the good behavior you have asked for. While clicker training isn't the only method you can use, it is a very effective one. You can even combine the use of a clicker with other positive training methods to enhance them.

6. Long line

If you want to start practicing off-leash behaviors, but you're not confident enough that your dog will follow you, then you may use a long line. This is a simple and safe alternative you can use before completely taking the leash off during training. Also, you can use a long line to allow your dog to explore without you or allow them extra room for scent detection and other activities. Most long lines vary between 15 and 30 feet in length.

7. Training treats

Training isn't fun without treats! In some cases, using treats makes training more effective too. There are many different types of dog treats available for dogs, but as mentioned in the previous section, you can also opt for high-value treats to make your dog feel more motivated. Vary the treats you use depending on the behavior or trick you are trying to train. Also, use different types of treats so that your dog doesn't get bored with the rewards.

8. **Training belt or treat pouch**

    While you can cram all of your dog's treats in your pocket to keep them on-hand for training, where will you put the rest of your tools and training items? Besides, you don't want all the other dogs to start following you around because you smell like treats, right? Using a training belt or treat pouch will help you out immensely as you can keep all of your items inside one. Opt for one that's odor-resistant and washable so that you can clean it as needed. There are belts or pouches that even have extra pockets for your personal items, such as your keys, phone, and wallet. You may also use a bigger container or bag to store the rest of your training equipment, including toys, treats, and comfort items.

9. **Toys**

    Apart from treats and praises, toys also serve as great rewards for dogs in training. To ensure the effectiveness of the reward, get to know your dog better. That way, you can purchase toys that you know your dog will be interested in. Keep these favorite toys on-hand during training sessions to reward your dog for a job well done.

10. **Barriers**

    These include pet pens, pet gates, playpens, and crates. These barriers are very useful for when you want to keep your dog in a single space for chewing management, house training, and other training methods. You can also use barriers to keep your dog away from problem areas like doors, stairs, and more.

Basic Commands and How to Teach Them

The feelings of joy, love, and fulfillment that your dog will bring into your life is incomparable. Unlike most people, dogs will love you unconditionally. But without training, don't expect your dog to know exactly how to behave at home or in other environments. Training teaches your dog how to behave well while ensuring their safety. Although it's ideal for dogs to learn early on, even older dogs can be taught with the proper training. When it comes to training, there are a few basic commands your dog must learn before you can move on to the more advanced stuff. These basic commands are:

Fig. 5: Dog Sitting. From Unsplash, by Spring Fed Images,

Sit

This command is one of the easiest to teach your dog, which is why most beginners start with this one.

- While your dog is standing, take a treat and hold it right next to their nose. Whenever you start teaching commands, make sure to do so in a calm manner.
- Slowly move the treat up so that your dog's head follows the treat. When this happens, your dog's bottom will lower. If needed, push down your dog's bottom for them to sit down.

- Once your dog is in position, give the command "Sit." Give the command firmly and clearly. Then, give your dog the treat and praise them for a job well done.

Keep doing these steps a couple of times each day until your dog can sit on command without your assistance. Then, start asking your dog to sit each time you want them to calm down—like before you leave the house, before eating meals, and more.

Stay

You can only try this command out once your dog has mastered "Sit." This is because the command starts with your dog in a sitting position.

- Start by asking your dog to "Sit." Most tricks begin with this command, which is why you should teach "Sit" first.
- Hold your palm out in front of your dog's face, then give the command "Stay." Again, say the command firmly and gently.
- Take a couple of steps back to see if your dog will, in fact, stay. If your dog stays, give them a treat as a reward.
- Each time you practice this trick, try increasing the number of steps you take away from your dog before you give a reward. Keep rewarding your pooch for staying in place no matter how brief they stay.

This is one command that exercises your dog's self-control. If your dog keeps going to you, especially at the beginning, don't feel discouraged. This is especially true for dogs who have a lot of energy and for puppies.

Come

This is an important command that helps keep your canine out of trouble. Ideally, when you give the command, this will bring your dog back to you.

- For this command, you need to attach the leash to your dog's collar to ensure that they don't run away from you.
- Go down to your dog's level and give the command "Come" as you pull on their leash gently. Strengthen the command by looking your dog in the eyes.
- If your dog comes to you, give them a treat as soon as they reach you.

Keep repeating these steps until your dog has mastered the command. Then, take the leash off and see if your dog will follow you. When training off-leash, make sure to do it in an enclosed area to keep your dog safe.

Heel

This is another important command wherein you teach your dog to walk alongside you rather than walking in front of you. While you walk with your dog, their head would be in line with your knees. This is an excellent command that teaches your dog to walk on a leash properly.

- For this command, you need to attach the leash to your dog's collar. Start off by asking your dog to "Sit."
- Hold your dog's leash with one hand and hold a squeaky toy above your dog's head with the other hand.
- While keeping the toy in position, start walking while you give the command "Heel." Don't rush this step as it might cause your dog to get excited.
- Press the squeaky toy to catch the attention of your dog while you are walking so that they start following you.

- If, at any point, your dog pulls in front of you or gets distracted, stop walking.
- When your dog's attention goes back to you, give the toy to them along with praises.
- After about half a minute of focusing on you, start walking once again.
- The more you practice, lengthen the time your dog walks with you before you give them a reward.

Practice this command daily to make it easier for you to take your dog out for walks. Over time, you may be able to walk with your dog even without a leash.

Down

As far as basic commands go, this is one of the more difficult ones to teach, mainly because it places your dog in a submissive posture. To make things easier for you and your canine companion, maintain a relaxed and positive tone while teaching this command. This is particularly important for anxious or fearful dogs from shelters.

- To start off, select a treat that has a particularly good smell, place it in your palm, and close your first around it.
- Hold your fist up to the snout of your dog. As soon as you see that your dog is interested (meaning they start sniffing your fist), slowly move your fist down, allowing your dog to follow.
- Gently slide your fist along the floor in front of your dog so that their body starts following their head. This will naturally cause your dog's body to slide down to the floor.
- Once down, give the command "Down," and give your dog a treat and some good words too.

As with the other commands on our list, it's best to practice this everyday. In cases where your dog lunges to you or tries to sit up, take away your fist and firmly say "No." You don't have to push your dog into position. Just follow these steps to encourage your dog to do it themselves.

Leave it

If you want to ensure your dog's safety, this is one of the best basic commands to teach them. Dogs are very curious, and they tend to sniff or paw at things they find interesting, even though these things may cause them harm. For this command, your goal is to let them learn that they will get a reward for leaving something (possibly dangerous) behind.

- Place treats in both of your hands.
- Show your dog one of the treats, close your fist around it, and present your fist to them. Give the command "Leave it." Of course, your dog won't leave it alone!
- If your dog tries to sniff, paw, lick, bark, or mouth your fist to get the treat, ignore these behaviors. Remember not to give attention to negative behaviors!
- Once your dog stops trying to get the treat, give them the treat from your other hand.
- Keep practicing this until your dog immediately moves away from your fist with a treat when you give the command.
- Once your dog masters this, you can improve it by only giving them a treat when they move away and look up at you.

Once you see that your dog has gained mastery of this command, you can modify the steps to take things up a notch.

- For this part, you need two kinds of treats: a "standard" treat and a high-value treat.
- Place the standard treat on the floor, cover it using your hand, and say the command "Leave it." Since this is a variation of the normal steps, your dog might show interest in the treat on the floor.
- If your dog tries to sniff, paw, lick, bark or mouth your hand to get the treat, ignore these behaviors. Once your dog stops trying to get the treat and looks up at you, take your hand off the treat, remove it, and give your dog the high-value treat right away.
- After this, you can take it even further. Place the standard treat on the floor while only covering it partially with your hand while you say the command "Leave it."
- Again, if your dog tries to sniff, paw, lick, bark, or mouth to get the treat, ignore these behaviors.
- Once your dog stops trying to get the treat and looks up at you, uncover the treat, remove it, and give your dog the high-value treat right away.

As time goes by, uncover the treat on the floor little by little until you have uncovered it completely, and your dog doesn't try to get it when you give the command. Upon mastery, you can try doing this while you are standing up. For this, repeat the same steps—but if your dog tries to get the treat, use your foot to cover it up while saying "No."

Get off

This command is essential to keep your dog off the furniture or off the bed. While it's not as common as the other commands, it's still considered a basic command because you may have to do it constantly, especially if you want to prevent getting pet hair on your furniture.

- If you see your pooch on your bed, sofa or any other piece of furniture, say the command "Get off" or simply "Off" while encouraging them to approach you.
- If your dog gets off, calmly reward then with a treat and some praise. If not, physically guide your dog off while saying the command.

For this command, teach the other members of your household to do it too. Consistency is key, especially for this particular command. So, when they see your dog sitting or lying in a place they aren't supposed to be, your family members should also give the "Get off" command.

Chapter 3: Training Puppies

When you take a puppy home, they won't come with an understanding of your rules or your language. A puppy is like a blank slate with natural instincts and behaviors. If you want your puppy to grow up to become a well-behaved dog, you must put in the time and effort to train them. Within the first month of bringing your puppy home, consult with a veterinarian for a wellness exam. This gives you a chance to get the first or second round of vaccinations for your pup, depending on whether your little dog has already had vaccinations or not.

Each time you go to the vet with your puppy, bring high-value treats to calm them down and make them feel happier. After the first round of vaccines, you can start off with your puppy training. Widen your pup's world a bit more by taking them to safe locations for socialization. Some examples of such places are dog training centers (make sure that these are clean and well-managed), local shops or restaurants, your neighbor's house, and public parks. However, if your puppy hasn't had their complete vaccinations yet, stay away from places that have a high likelihood of dog traffic. When it comes to puppies, you have up to 12 weeks to provide them with positive exposure to and experiences with the human world as this is when their brains are still developing.

Since you are likely to be bringing your puppy home when they are about 8 weeks old, that only gives you about 4 weeks to provide as much positive exposure as possible. The very first month of your puppy's life with you is when you should gradually introduce them to different kinds of people, different environments, other dogs (both young and old), and car rides. As much as possible, introduce your tiny dog to several new stimuli throughout the day—at least 5 would be ideal. After introducing these new stimuli, keep exposing your puppy to them while pairing the experience with a treat or some other fun activity. Just don't force your puppy into things that make them feel anxious or scared. When you go into a new environment (a safe one, of course), allow your puppy to greet it with enthusiasm and with their natural urge to explore, run, and sniff at everything. This will help build confidence and resilience in your pup.

Another thing you must teach your puppy within the first month is that your touch—and the touch of the other members of your household—is something comforting, not threatening. If you have brought home a puppy who has been abused or one who hasn't been cared for during the first weeks of their life, convincing them that touch is a good thing may take more time. But just keep your touches gentle, affectionate, comforting, and loving so that your puppy will eventually look forward to them.

From the second to the fourth month of your puppy's life, you can start house-training them. Fortunately, around this age, house-training comes quite easily as they are naturally programmed to eliminate in one place. Make sure to prepare a safe place for your puppy to do their business—a place that smells and seems familiar to them. Throughout the process of house-training, maintaining consistency is key. Also, you may want to start indoors first before teaching your puppy to do their business outdoors. Keep the rewards coming as you house-train your dog until they learn how to do it on their own. If your puppy has any accidents while you are training them, don't punish them for it. When it comes to your puppy's bodily functions, try not to do anything that will cause a negative association with them. Just stay calm, assertive, and quiet as you bring your puppy to where they should do their business.

When it comes to puppy training, there are so many things for you to learn and teach to your tiny dog. Let's go through the fundamental and practical tips for puppy training to arm you with the knowledge you need to train your new companion successfully.

How Early Should You Start?

Just like babies, puppies are delightful bundles of joy, curiosity, and energy. But a lot of times, they can also be very frustrating and exasperating. As an owner, it is up to you to deal with all of the challenges of training puppies—and the more knowledgeable and patient you are, the shorter your adjustment period will be. This adjustment period will be a lot less stressful too.

After you bring your puppy home (able to leave their mother at 8 weeks old), allow him or her to settle into your home—which is a new environment for them—first before starting with your training. If you have taken or bought your puppy from a good breeder or shelter, they may have started the socializing part of your training already. If not, then it's time for you to catch up. For puppies, keep in mind that their attention spans are very short, so don't make your training sessions too long. But by 8 weeks old and above, you can start teaching your puppy the most basic commands (the ones we went through in the previous chapter).

When you start training your puppy at 8 weeks old, only use positive reinforcement training methods along with a lot of gentle encouragement. Schedule short training sessions for your puppy, but make sure to have them every day. Integrate your training sessions throughout the day—at least 15 minutes per session will suffice. This means that you can have 3 sessions of 5 minutes long throughout the day. If you share your home with others, you can ask them to take turns with you in training your puppy. Also, train your puppy in different locations around your home to make them feel more relaxed and comfortable as they grow up.

If you want to have a well-behaved, well-trained dog in the future, make a commitment to reinforce your puppy's training daily, especially for their first year of life. Determine the training method to use for teaching the basic commands to your dog. Once you have taught these basic commands, keep practicing them every chance you get. For instance, before you give your puppy their meal, ask them to "Sit" while you prepare the food. Or before you go out with your puppy, ask them to get "Down" while waiting for you. That way, you will be able to build a routine for your puppy to help them learn what is expected of them. When it comes to practicing the basic commands, be as creative as possible. It's helpful for you to think about the rules and routines you want your puppy to follow first. That way, you will have a guide for when you are training your puppy to learn them.

Coming Up with a Training Schedule for Your Puppy

Coming up with a training schedule for your puppy is as easy as coming up with a schedule for your tasks for the day, whether at home or at work. The important thing is to create a structured schedule so that you can teach your puppy what they should do while living in your home. For the first few weeks (and months) of your puppy's life, here are the things to include in your training schedule:

When your puppy is 8 weeks old

As previously mentioned, the earlier you start training your puppy, the better. Before you bring your puppy home, you should have already prepared yourself and your home for basic puppy training. That way, all you have to do is execute your plans. Here are some things to include in your puppy training schedule:

- **Household rules**

    It's important to teach your puppy the behaviors that are allowed in your home and those that aren't. When it comes to household rules, here are some things to include in your training and training schedule:

    - Train your puppy that "Yes" means that you like the behavior they are doing.
    - Train your puppy that "No" means they should

stop doing the behavior.
- Train your puppy to go inside their crate and remain there quietly when you close the door.
- Train your puppy to go to bed at the same time each night (around the same time as you go to bed).
- Train your puppy to go out at the same time each morning.
- Train your puppy to know where their grooming spot is—where you brush your puppy's fur, where you clip your puppy's nails, where you clean your puppy's teeth, and so on.

- **Feeding routines**

Fig. 6: Feeding. From Pixabay, by Martina

To make it easier for your puppy to learn, make sure that their water and food bowls remain in one place. Puppies learn better with routines, meaning repetitiveness, predictability, and familiarity. Therefore, when teaching things to your puppy, try to do the same thing each day using the same order of events and the same commands or words. Here is an effective way to build a feeding routine with your puppy:

- When you're about to prepare the meal for your puppy, give them a cue by asking a question like, "Do you want your FOOD now?" No matter how you compose your command, make sure to exaggerate the most important words for your puppy to remember them.

- Allow your puppy to accompany you to the kitchen, where you ask them to "Sit."
- Get your puppy's food bowl from the same place, then set it in the same place each time. As you prepare your dog's food, you will be watched intently. Following the same routine for preparation teaches your dog that you are their food source.
- If your puppy isn't sitting down or if they are acting too excitable, don't set the food bowl in front of them. Otherwise, your pup will learn that excitable behavior makes food appear! Instead, allow your puppy to calm down first before giving them the food bowl.

Teaching your puppy to sit before giving their food bowl encourages patience and calmness, two essential traits to make the process of training smoother and easier. Once your puppy has started eating, don't approach them. Tell the other members of your household to do the same. Other pets shouldn't approach your eating puppy either. If your puppy walks away without finishing the food in their bowl, make a note of this; it may be an indication that your puppy is ill. If it happens frequently, consult with a vet. After about 10 minutes, pick up your dog's bowl. This helps prevent the development of food guarding or picky eating habits.

Wrap up your puppy's feeding routine by having a potty break right after each meal. If you are in the process of housebreaking your puppy, take them out on a leash.

Make sure to announce the activity first before you take your dog out by saying something like, "It's time to go OUT!" Follow this kind of feeding routine each day for your dog to learn it quickly.

- **Crate-training**

Crates are an invaluable tool for puppy training as they help protect your puppy from household dangers, help you with housebreaking, and give your puppy a safe place to settle in and relax. In other words, your puppy's crate is their own secure and safe den. While your puppy might, at first, feel unhappy because their movements get restricted, the more you encourage the use of the crate, the more your puppy will get used to it. Soon, you will notice that your puppy is entering the crate on their own to rest, take naps, or simply escape from the hustle and bustle of your household.

As soon as your puppy gets used to their crate, it will be easier for you to take them along for car rides and trips to the vet. You should also make sure to keep your puppy inside the crate when you are not there to supervise them directly. This is especially true if you haven't housebroken your puppy yet. Otherwise, you might find a lot of surprises all around your home. Crate training is important because puppies shouldn't be given too much freedom. Pups who are left loose around the house can either develop bad habits or end up getting hurt.

When your puppy is 9 weeks old

As your puppy reaches 9 weeks, continue including the previous routines in your puppy's schedule to reinforce them. Apart from these, you must also teach your puppy the following:

- **More basic rules**

  To make it easier for you and your dog to live together in harmony, you should introduce basic rules little by little. Other rules to introduce to your puppy starting when they are 9 weeks old include the following:

  - Train your puppy to remain calm while indoors. This reduces the likelihood of developing behavior problems. Don't allow a lot of jumping, barking, rough play, running around, and other disruptive behaviors.
  - Train your puppy not to nip or mouth at your feet or hands—or anyone else's.
  - Train your puppy to gently take toys and food from your hand. If your puppy tries to grab things from you, don't give in.
  - Train your puppy to be gentle by being gentle with them as well. You can also do this by being firm but gentle while you are correcting your puppy's behaviors.
  - Train your puppy how to interact with other people and pets. Train your puppy restraint, especially while playing with humans and other pets.
  - Train your puppy that jumping up on people—even you—isn't okay.

- Train your puppy to remain as still as possible while grooming.

- **Accept handling**

    As soon as you bring your puppy home, start handling them immediately. This makes it easier for your puppy to accept the things you need to do with them. Make sure that your puppy accepts the fact that you are the leader, and therefore, you make the decisions about which behaviors are okay and which behaviors aren't.

    When you are handling your puppy, do so gently. The more you handle your puppy, the more they will come to accept that everything you are doing is for their own good. As part of handling, you must also train your dog to respect any other pets you have at home. Your puppy shouldn't take anything away from other pets nor should they show jealousy, pushiness, bickering, pestering, or other negative behaviors.

When your puppy is 10 weeks old

At 10 weeks old, continue practicing the training and commands you have already introduced. Apart from these, include the following in your training schedule:

- Train your puppy to learn how to walk with a leash without pulling you. If your dog continues pulling on the leash when you take walks, train them to stop this behavior first before you continue taking walks.
- Train your puppy to wait in front of open gates and doors until you give them permission to go through.

- Train your puppy to come when you call. This is one of the more important commands to teach your puppy.
- Train your puppy to bark only when appropriate.

When your puppy is 12 weeks old

When your puppy has reached 12 weeks of age, continue with your training. By this time, your puppy should already be well on their way to becoming a well-rounded dog. But you're not done yet; there is still a lot to learn. As you continue with your puppy training, you want to include the following:

- Train your puppy to remain seated until you have given a command for them to get up.
- Train your puppy to get into their crate or bed when you give the command and remain there until you give them permission to get up.

Basically, this is the time when you train your dog to control their impulses, to remain calm, and to encourage both mental and physical relaxation. If you have been training your puppy since the beginning, your pup will be able to learn these things more easily.

When your puppy is 16 weeks old

At 16 weeks old, keep on training and reinforcing the things your puppy has already learned. This is also the time when you can introduce the following:

- Train your puppy to pay attention to you and stay close

to you while you take structured walks.
- Train your puppy to either greet other people and animals politely or simply ignore them. If your puppy acts aggressively, fearfully or excitably, don't allow this.
- Train your puppy to play with different kinds of toys. As much as possible, introduce a variety of toys to your puppy to determine which types they like the most and which ones they aren't too keen on. Toys keep your puppy busy, stimulated, and happy. They can also be used as part of positive reinforcement training methods.
- Potty-train your puppy. This is one of the most challenging things to teach young dogs, but it is essential. Create a separate schedule for potty-training your dog wherein you take them out as soon as they wake up in the morning, after meals, after nap time, and right before going to bed. It's much easier to potty train puppies when you create and stick to a potty-training schedule.

Now that you know more about what to include in your puppy's training schedule, you can start creating your own. But even if you make a schedule, if you see that something isn't working or you think that your puppy isn't ready to learn some of the things we have discussed here, make adjustments as needed. Don't force your puppy to do things they aren't ready for as this might make training a negative experience for them.

Potty-Training Your Puppy

Potty-training puppies requires a lot of patience, positive

reinforcement, and consistency. Your main goal here is to bond with your pup while teaching them good habits. Normally, it would take between 4 and 6 months before you can fully potty-train your puppy. For some puppies, it may take longer. In particular, smaller dog breeds have higher metabolisms and smaller bladders, meaning that you will have to take them outside more frequently.

Another factor that might have an effect on the length of time you would be able to start potty-training your puppy is their past living conditions. If during their first 8 weeks of life, your puppy was never introduced to the concept of potty-training, you will first have to break their old habits before teaching new ones. If you experience any setbacks while training, don't let them bring you down. Just maintain your potty-training program to provide your pup with the consistency they need to learn. Also, keep the praises and rewards coming so that your puppy will always feel motivated to follow you.

According to experts, you may start potty-training your pup when he or she reaches the age of 12 weeks. By this age, puppies already have sufficient control of their bowel movements and bladder, making it easier for them to learn how to hold it in. If you bring home a puppy who is over 12 weeks old and who is used to eliminating inside their crate or cage, expect the process to take longer. But you can always reshape the behavior of your puppy with rewards and encouragement.

When it comes to potty-training puppies, a lot of pet owners start training indoors. This is especially true for those who don't have yards or for puppies who haven't received all of their shots yet. Start potty-training indoors then gradually transition your puppy to going outdoors. For indoor potty-training, one of the best ways to train your puppy is with the use of puppy pads. First, determine the space where you will start potty-training your pup. A laundry room, bathroom or any other confined area with floors that are easy to clean would be ideal. Also, make sure that you puppy-proof the space first to ensure the safety of your little dog. Then, set up a space on the floor by covering it with pee pads and placing the bed of your puppy in the corner. Here are some steps to guide you as you start your puppy's potty-training routine:

- Change the pee pads regularly. But it's also helpful to place a small piece of a soiled pad atop the padded area where you want your pup to pee. The purpose of this is to provide your puppy with a scent to remind them that this is the area where they have to go potty. Change the soiled pad regularly too so that it doesn't start decomposing on the spot.
- When you notice that your puppy has learned how to go potty in one area, you can start removing the pads right next to their bed.
- Over time, you can gradually remove more and more pee pads until you are left with 1 or 2 sheets placed in the area where your puppy usually goes potty on.
- If your puppy constantly goes potty on the remaining pee pads, you may extend their areas of access gradually. But if your puppy starts having accidents, reduce that area once again.

After successfully potty-training your puppy indoors, it's time to start training them to do their business outside. To do this, the first thing you need to teach your puppy is the "potty cue." This is an important part of the training as it serves as a signal to go potty. Your goal here is to show your pet how to use the potty cue to tell you that they need to go outside. Here are some steps to help you transition from going potty indoors to going potty outdoors:

- **Teach the potty cue to your puppy**

    First, bring your puppy by the door and give them the command to "Sit." Then, you can either teach your puppy to bark, ring a bell, or scratch the door if they want to go out. At first, you may have to demonstrate this. The potty cue is simply a signal that your puppy wants to go out to do their business, so you shouldn't use it when you're just taking your pup out to play. When your puppy performs the cue you taught, open the door, let them out, and give them a treat. You can think of your own potty cue. When it comes to this signal, you decide what you want it to be.

- **Determine your puppy's potty area**

    Before you take your dog out, place them on a leash. This is an especially important step so that your dog knows that after the potty cue, taking them outside has a specific purpose. Take your puppy to the area that you have set as their potty area and stop there. Patiently wait until your puppy has done their business. After that, reward your puppy with treats and praises. This makes the whole experience a positive one so that your puppy will look forward to doing it again. But if your puppy doesn't do their business, bring your puppy back inside your house, then repeat the process. Over time, your puppy will learn what these actions mean.

- **When your puppy is left alone at home, leave them in their crate**

    Unless you have fully potty-trained your puppy, you

should keep them inside their crate when leaving them home alone. This will help prevent accidents in the different parts of your home while you aren't there. If they were to have an accident while they were home alone, you wouldn't be able to correct your puppy's behavior.

As you build and strengthen your puppy's potty routine, make sure to show your pup a lot of love and encouragement. Don't make the experience a negative or scary one as this might end up teaching your puppy the wrong things. Also, don't punish your puppy for not learning things as quickly as you want them to. Simply correct the behaviors as needed. Remember... patience is key!

Practical Tips for Training Puppies

Fig. 7: Puppy Training. From Unsplash, by Jairo

Starting off on the right foot (or paw) with your puppy makes them feel more secure in your home and in your presence. To continue providing good experiences to your pup, use positive reinforcement methods as a foundation for your puppy training. Consistent, gentle, and loving puppy training provides you with a strong foundation for your relationship with your puppy. When you start early, you will be able to live with your puppy peacefully and without (much) stress. Teaching your dog to learn what is expected of them from the beginning will have a positive impact on the healthy growth and development of your young canine companion. To wrap up this chapter on puppy training, here are some more practical tips for you to use:

- **Research how puppies learn**

    Reading this book about dog training is an excellent way to learn more about dogs and learning. When you have a puppy, you can think of them as a clean slate. With the proper guidance and learning techniques, your puppy can become whatever you want them to be. To reinforce what you learn here, you can also talk to professional dog trainers and ask them for advice. Learning everything you can about training puppies and dogs of all ages equips you with the knowledge you need to ensure training success.

- **Set clear boundaries from the start**

    No matter how cute your puppy is, you should set clear boundaries for them and enforce these boundaries. Of course, this doesn't mean that you should be overly strict with your puppy. Train, educate, and be as firm as needed, but whenever your puppy does a good job or learns the behavior you want them to learn, shower your pup with love, praises, and treats.

- **Make sure you give signals explicitly and commands clearly**

    Puppies are very good when it comes to reading your

facial expressions. They will often react quickly when you give simple commands or simple hand signals compared to complex sentences or signals. This is why the basic commands only consist of 1 or 2 words. It's much easier for your puppy to learn these commands when you make them as simple, as clear, and as explicit as possible.

- **Develop your puppy's social skills early on**

  For the first five to six months of your puppy's life, try to introduce them to a hundred different people or so. This makes your puppy comfortable in the company of others, not just you. To make this even better, bring a small bag filled with your puppy's favorite treats with you and ask the people your puppy meets to feed them treats. This teaches your puppy not to feel threatened by other human beings.

  If you have the resources, you may also consider enrolling your puppy in kindergarten class so that they can play with other dogs while learning essential social skills. Puppies should learn how to interact with all other living things around them for them to grow up to be happy, healthy, and well-balanced.

- **When you take your puppy to new places, make it a fun experience**

  While your puppy is still young, don't focus too much on obedience training; you can do this type of training later on. But when it comes to socialization and exploration, these must be done while your puppy is still young. They will have an impact on how your puppy's temperament will be when they grow up. When taking your puppy to new places to meet other people or animals, make each experience fun. This will help prevent the development of fear or aggression issues along with other kinds of behavioral problems when your puppy grows into an adult.

- **Your puppy training should include walking on a leash**

    Obvious as this tip might seem, many dog owners neglect this until their puppies have already grown into young or adult dogs. But training your puppy to respectfully and calmly walk on a leash can help you with other training methods, such as potty-training and socializing.

- **Understand your puppy's natural guarding instinct**

    Puppies are naturally inclined to protect their toys, food, friends, and everything else they hold dear. When you notice your puppy having fun with something or someone, taking this away will teach your puppy to guard them instead of giving them up. If you want your puppy to let go of something, distract them with another object before you take it away.

- **Don't use your puppy's crate as punishment**

    You want your puppy to love their crate and feel comfortable in it. But once you start using it as a form of punishment, your puppy will hate the crate—and this is very difficult to unlearn. Using any form of punishment (this differs from discipline, which we will be going through later on) might have detrimental effects on your training, especially when it comes to puppies.

- **Your puppy training should include learning not to bite, nip, or mouth**

    While your puppy is still young, teach them that biting isn't okay. If your puppy nips at you or bites you a bit too hard, say "Ouch!" using the same pitch as a puppy's yelp when their tail or foot is stepped on. This serves as a warning that what your puppy did wasn't a good thing. If you see that your puppy listens (meaning they stop biting you), give them a treat or praise them. You can also choose to ignore the behavior, then turn around and tuck your hands under your armpits. This is a calming signal for puppies and dogs.

- **Gain your puppy's trust so that you can establish a strong bond**

    As much as you love your puppy, he or she should also love and trust you in return. But you cannot simply demand this love and trust; you must work hard to earn it. Once you have gained their trust, it will serve as the foundation of your bond. The more you treat your puppy the right way, the stronger your bond becomes. With this strong bond, your puppy will want to please you all the time, thus making training easier.

- **Encourage your puppy to explore**

    The more you allow and encourage your puppy to explore their surroundings, the more confident they become. You can also encourage your puppy to explore different objects both at home and in different surroundings. Finally, encourage your puppy to explore and interact with people and other dogs (even other pets if you have them at home). All of this exploration helps your puppy develop into a well-rounded and well-balanced dog.

- **Your puppy training should include teaching your puppy how to stay home by themselves**

    When you leave your puppy at home, they will feel very stressed. Of course, you can't bring your pup everywhere you go, right? Therefore, you should train your puppy to remain inside their crate while you are out. This is why it's important to get your puppy used to their crate. The more relaxed and comfortable they are, the easier it will be to leave your puppy home alone. You may also want to leave a toy in your puppy's crate to keep them entertained. Just make sure that the toy you leave is something your puppy is interested in and is something safe.

    Positive reinforcement works when you're trying to train your puppy to stay home alone. You can place your puppy's crate in a room, then leave them there for some time. If your puppy doesn't make a fuss while you left them alone, reward them for it. Then, you can increase the length of time that you leave your puppy to help them learn that they will be okay even if you're not around.

- **Introduce new words to your puppy and keep expanding their vocabulary**

    As previously mentioned, puppies aren't born with an understanding of English vocabulary (or any other language for that matter). If you want your pup to learn what specific commands mean, it's your responsibility to teach them—and you should do this right away. Talk to your puppy frequently to strengthen your bond. Share your experiences through words. Over time, this will help your puppy learn what words mean. This might even make it easier for your puppy to learn commands once you start puppy training.

- **Provide guidance and encouragement for your puppy instead of trying to control them**

    The key to successful puppy training is not to control, force, or coerce your puppy into doing what you want. Instead, provide your puppy with a lot of love, encouragement, praise, rewards, and guidance to make the experience more positive. This is especially important for puppies so that they won't grow up fearing or resenting you.

Chapter 4: Training Young Dogs

While most people prefer to adopt puppies, you may end up with a dog who is a bit older. After reading the last chapter, you might be thinking, "How do I go about this now?" The good news is that when it comes to training dogs, you can start at any age and stage!

Before you bring your young dog home, try to find out all you can about their earlier weeks or months of life. Did your young dog experience any prior training? Was your young dog able to socialize and explore adequately? Has potty or crate-training been introduced to your young dog? These are important questions to ask your source to determine where you should start with your training.

Ideally, though, whether your young dog has already experienced training in the past, you will want to start at the beginning. Your young dog will be used to the routines of the place where they grew up. But you will have your own routines at home, and your dog must learn these. To catch up with your dog's training, come up with a training schedule for each day and stick with it, no excuses.

You may want to start with potty-training as this would already be considered "delayed." Follow the same steps that we have discussed in the previous chapter for potty-training puppies. Depending on the past experiences your young dog had in terms of training, this may either be very easy or very challenging. But this is one skill you must train your dog to do as part of their discipline. Then, you can start expanding your dog's vocabulary, teaching the basic commands, and more. Also, don't forget to shower your dog with love, affection, encouragement, and rewards to make your young dog happy, healthy, and well-adjusted.

Learning from Older Dogs

Have you ever heard of "allelomimetic behaviors?"

It sounds strange, doesn't it?

But this concept is actually very important when it comes to other dogs. Allelomimetic behaviors are a type of group-coordinated behavior. They depend on dogs' natural inclination to follow, imitate, and want to be in the company of other dogs. You can use this knowledge to help your young dog (or even your puppies) learn the proper behaviors. Allowing your young dog to socialize with older, well-trained dogs will help them learn a lot of essential behaviors, especially those that are socially significant.

Fig. 8: Dogs Learning. From Pixabay. by

If this is your first time attempting to train a dog, and you have a young dog, you can reinforce, simplify, or improve your training by allowing them to spend time with older dogs. Once your young dog has gotten used to these older dogs, you will start noticing the allelomimetic behaviors. For instance, if the owner of the older dog tells their dog to "Come," the dog will obey... and trailing behind that dog will be your own. In the same way, when your young dog is able to watch older dogs being trained, they will have a better idea of what is expected of them once you start with their training.

This type of learning can be extremely effective when done right. If you want your young dog to learn from older dogs, find friends or family members who have already trained their own dogs successfully. Then you can start scheduling "play dates" for your dogs for the purpose of enjoyment, socialization, and education. The more you find ways to make dog training easier, the higher your chance of success will be. As far as ease and convenience go, this method is a winner!

Top Tips for Training Young Dogs

As challenging as dog training is, it can also be one of the most rewarding and fun aspects of raising a young dog. As soon as you bring your small dog home, make dog training one of your top priorities. Dogs are very trainable, even if they've grown beyond the puppy stage. Even professional dog trainers will accept dogs of all ages, breeds, and abilities. Of course, we have already discussed the added benefits of training your dog on your own. It helps strengthen your bond with your dog, and it also helps you learn more about your dog too.

For dog training, the most effective methods are those based on rewards or positive reinforcement. When you give your young dog toys, praise, or treats that they really like, this will help make your training much easier. Since you will be training your dog yourself, you will be able to determine exactly what motivates them. Yes, you will experience struggles and failures while training your dog, but don't let that stop you. Keep moving forward by learning more about your dog and using these helpful tips for training your young one:

1. **When setting and enforcing rules, maintain consistency**

    It cannot be said enough: consistency is extremely important when it comes to dog training, especially in terms of setting rules and enforcing them. Make sure that each day, every day, your dog follows the rules that you have set. If there are other people living in your home, make sure that they enforce these rules too. This means that you may have to teach them how to train your young dog (or let them read this book too!) so that they know what needs to be done. While you will be doing the introductions and most of the teaching, the other members of your household should help with the reinforcement. This consistency will help your young dog understand their role at home and what is considered acceptable and unacceptable behavior.

2. **Maintain consistency with your words too**

    While young dogs may already understand a few words, this doesn't mean that they have an adequate vocabulary already. Therefore, it's your responsibility to teach them. You may talk to your dog about things around you and the experiences you have. But when it comes to training and teaching commands, use the same words over and over again. For instance, when you're training your dog to "Sit," don't say "Sit" one time, then "Sit down" the next. This will just end up confusing your canine companion.

3. Be aware of the limitations of your young dog

The best way to make yourself aware of your dog's limitations (and abilities) is by learning about their past from your source. If you acquired your dog from a shelter or a breeder, you can interview the people who took care of your young dog first. Then, compare what you have learned with what you observe while interacting with and training your dog.

On the other hand, if you acquired your dog from a rescue shelter or you decided to adopt a stray, you may have to do a lot of observing and experimenting to determine your dog's limitations. Either way, learning what your dog can and cannot do will help you customize your training methods.

4. Encourage and reinforce the good behaviors of your young dog

If you want to have a well-behaved, happy dog, shower them with encouragement, praise, rewards, and other good things. This is why positive reinforcement training methods are recommended instead of methods that incorporate harsh words and punishments. Think about it; when you constantly shout at your dog and hit them, how will they learn good behaviors?

While you are observing your dog, praise them for doing good things no matter how small or ordinary those good things are. Doing this will help reinforce their behavior when you are training your dog. When you praise, encourage, or reward your dog during training, they will remember the times when you did the same thing. Over time, your young dog will start learning the behaviors that bring about these reactions from you.

5. Consider your young dog's environment while training

No matter what age your dog is, you must always consider the environment where you are training them. This is especially important when you are introducing new commands or tricks. Perform your training in an environment free of distractions to improve your success. Conversely, if you try to train in a new environment or in a place that makes your dog excited, you might see your training session go to waste. Think about the training you have planned and choose the appropriate environment for it.

6. Don't expect to be a perfect dog trainer

For a lot of dog trainers, when they make mistakes, they stop dead in their tracks. They take this as a sign that they aren't meant to train their dog or that they don't have the right skills for the task. Don't be too hard on yourself. If you make mistakes, learn from them. Make adjustments to your training methods to prevent those mistakes from happening again. There is no such thing as a perfect dog trainer, not even among professionals. We all make mistakes, we all have our triumphs, and we can always learn new things along the way. If you feel like you're struggling, try to learn more about your young dog. You can also ask for help. Just don't give up on dog training entirely!

7. **Customize your training methods to suit the needs and abilities of your young dog**

   The great thing about dog training is that it's completely flexible. Although there are basic commands and effective ways to teach them, you can customize your training method to suit your own individual dog. For instance, while treats work for most dogs, your young dog might prefer praise or toys. So, even if you give them treats, they won't be motivated. Try to determine what your dog likes, what works, what doesn't work, and adjust your plans accordingly. This may seem intimidating at first, but over time, you will become a master of knowing how to train your dog in the best possible way.

8. **More training tips for you:**

   Apart from these tips, you can also apply the puppy training tips you have learned in the previous chapter. Depending on what your young dog already knows and what else you want to teach them, you may have to combine different methods to reach the goals you want your dog to achieve. Here are a few more tips for you:

   - Whether your dog already came with a name or you gave them one, use it consistently. That way, your dog will learn what their name is, and when you call it out, they will respond to you.
   - Patience is a virtue; always remember that. If you feel like you're not getting anywhere with your training session, stop. Do the same if you start feeling annoyed or frustrated with your dog. Also, keep in mind that dogs learn differently and at different rates. Remembering this fact may help extend your patience.

- Apart from the words you use, your dog can also understand your body movements and voice tone. Keep this in mind while training.
- Set short training sessions each day. This will prevent your dog from getting bored while training.
- Groom, stroke, pet, and handle your dog each day so that they get used to and accept being handled.
- Learning about and understanding your dog will help you predict their future behaviors and anticipate what they will do next.
- End all of your training sessions with a command or trick your dog already knows. This ensures that your training sessions always end on a positive note.

Chapter 5: Training Adult Dogs

Have you ever considered adopting an adult dog? A lot of people prefer adopting puppies and young dogs as they feel intimidated at the thought of adopting a dog that is all grown up—and the thing that intimidates them the most is the fact that they would have to train that grown-up dog. If this situation sounds familiar to you, don't let your fear stop you! There are so many adult dogs out there without homes, and the older they become, the closer they get to being euthanized... and that is just sad.

Even if you bring an adult dog into your home, it is entirely possible for you to train them. You might simply have to take a different approach than you would with puppies and young canines. But when it comes to the principles, training adult dogs is pretty much the same as training younger ones. And the older your dog is, the more patience you will need to train them. This is especially true if you have adopted a dog who has been abused, one who has never been trained, or one who has learned wrong or inappropriate behaviors. In some cases, you will first have to train your furry friend to unlearn the behaviors they have learned before you can start training them to do what's right. To start off, perform the following training with your dog:

Crate-Training

This type of training is essential, especially if you want house-training to become an easier task for you. Crate-training is a helpful and effective way to begin house-training your dog as it works with the natural instinct of canines not to do their business in their den. For most adult dogs, when they consider their crate as their den, they will try their best to "hold it in" as long as they are inside. But as soon as you notice that your dog needs to go, let them out immediately. We will go through more detailed steps for house-training your dog in the next section, but for now, here are some helpful pointers to keep in mind as you train your adult dog to get comfortable with their crate:

- Select a crate that your dog will fit into comfortably and one that you can clean and maintain easily.
- Train your dog to learn that they cannot access all the rooms of your home.
- Help your dog become more comfortable in their crate by establishing a routine that you follow each day.
- Take your dog outside for potty breaks. Do this about 4 to 5 times each day. If your dog doesn't do their business when you take them outdoors, that's okay. Just observe your dog carefully when you go back inside.
- Stock up on products for cleaning and removing stains of dog urine so that you can maintain the cleanliness of your dog's crate.
- If you aren't at home or you need to do something important while you are home, leave your dog in their crate.
- Observe your dog's behavior while inside to crate. This will help you determine whether your dog is merely whining to complain about being "trapped" inside the crate or they are truly feeling anxious about being left inside the crate on their own.
- To ease your dog's stress or anxiety, place 1 or 2 toys (preferably the indestructible ones) in with them to keep them entertained.

Be patient with crate-training and never force your dog to go inside their crate. Over time, you may start noticing that your dog goes into the crate even without prompting or rewards. When this happens, it means that they already feel comfortable in it.

Socialization

Important as this aspect of dog training is, a lot of dog owners end up neglecting it. This part of the training involves helping your dog feel comfortable in different kinds of social situations. This may be one of the more challenging things you will have to do if you adopt a rescue dog or one with a painful past. But if you are able to socialize your dog properly, you can transform your dog into a confident, friendly, and happy canine. Just make sure that you continue with socialization throughout your dog's lifetime to make it effective.

When it comes to socializing your dog, take things slow. As much as possible, follow your dog's pace and don't force them to interact or socialize with others right away. Also, don't attempt to push your canine out of their comfort zone at the beginning. You don't want to end up making your dog more fearful or anxious, right? As with other types of training, keep in mind that not all dogs learn in the same way or at the same rate. Your dog may find some people or situations easy to adjust to while they might also dislike some people or will refuse to go into certain environments.

Consider your dog's personality and past life too. If you obtained your canine from a breeder who cared for your dog well and trained them adequately, you may notice that socialization comes easily to them. On the other hand, if you obtained a dog from a shelter that saves dogs who have been abused or abandoned, you may notice that socialization isn't an easy thing to get used to.

Leash Training

Fig. 9: Leash Training, From Pixabay

There is one main difference that exists between leash-training adult dogs and leash-training puppies, and that is the amount of pain you will experience in your arm! Naturally, when a puppy pulls on a leash, the strain you will experience won't be as much as when an adult dog pulls on a leash, especially if you have chosen one of the bigger dog breeds. But when it comes to the principles and methods of leash training, these remain the same across all ages. Here are some tips to help you out:

- Prepare to correct your dog at each step of the process and try to increase your patience. It will be difficult, but not impossible.
- It's best to begin leash-training your dog at home before you take them to the park or to any other public place.
- If you want to gain control of your dog more effectively, purchase a high-quality training harness or collar for your canine companion. Just stay away from retractable leashes, as these have a tendency to be unpredictable.
- If you have a small or medium-sized canine, it would be best to use a simple collar with a chain-link design. But if you have a large or extra-large canine, it would be best to use a prong collar.
- If you have chosen to use a training collar, the right way to correct your dog is to give a "pop"—a sharp, short tug on your dog's leash to tighten their collar for a moment before releasing it just as quickly—on your dog's collar

while simultaneously giving a correction verbally.

- If you have chosen to use a prong collar, make the "pop" less sharp and shorter as this type of collar requires less pressure.
- If you have chosen to use a halter or harness, all you need to do is grip the leash firmly and apply gentle pressure for correction.
- When you are leash-training your dog, never yank at their neck or drag them forcefully because you might end up hurting them.

These are just some general tips for leash-training your adult dog. But when it comes to the actual training, here are some steps you can follow:

- Hold your dog's leash with one hand while your dog is on the opposite side of your body. In this starting position, your dog's leash should be running across your front while you also hold part of the leash with your other hand approximately at your thigh level.
- Give the command to "Sit" before you begin your walk. If you haven't taught this command yet, then simply allow your dog to stand next to you.
- Stay in this position for a few seconds to train your dog that it's time to take a walk. If your dog tries to lunge or walk forward, just give them a firm but gentle pop while saying "No" or "Wait." Only when your dog is able to stay in this position for at least 10 seconds (the longer, the better!), then you can take a step forward while giving the command, "Let's go."
- Take a short walk around your yard to give your dog practice. Whenever your dog lunges, yanks, pulls, or twists, stop walking while using verbal corrections simultaneously with pops to bring your dog back to you. Only when your dog stands still should you continue walking.

Perform leash-training with your dog daily. This will help your dog learn the correct behaviors for walking with you. When you see that your dog has learned how to walk on a leash properly, you may start experimenting by taking them on walks in other environments.

House-Training Adult Dogs

Depending on where you obtained your adult dog and how they were raised/trained until the time you brought the dog home, house-training may either be an easy or difficult task. Of course, a dog who has been trained in the past will only have to be taught where to do their business in or outside of your home. But if the dog you adopted has no prior training, then you will have to start from the very beginning as you would if you chose to adopt a puppy. For this aspect of training, here are the basic things to keep in mind:

Fig. 10: Housetraining. From Pixabay.

- **Observe your dog's behaviors first**

    From the time you bring your dog home, observe their potty-related behaviors. Try to see how frequently your dog does their business, the location where they usually do their business (if your dog only does their business in specific parts of the house), or if your dog only does their business under very specific conditions. For instance, your dog might pee when you call out their name in a firm way. This may indicate that they do this out of fear. Observing your dog will help you determine how to approach house-training.

- **Rule out medical conditions**

    If you notice that your dog does their business at inappropriate times or frequently does their business indoors as if they don't have control, consult with a vet first. Do this to rule out any medical conditions that might be causing your dog's potty-related behaviors. If your dog suffers from any medical condition, you can work with your vet to help them overcome it. If not, then you can start house-training your dog.

Make sure to include house-training in your dog training schedule. Do this as soon as you bring your dog home. Start observing, rule out medical conditions, then start your house-training. Here are some practical tips to do this successfully:

- Unless you actually caught your dog doing their business or having accidents anywhere in your house, don't punish them for it.
- If you catch your dog in the act, startle them with a clap or a shout, then bring them outdoors. Once your dog finishes their business, give them a reward or praise.
- Also, make sure to clean the mess your dog made in the house thoroughly so that they don't get attracted to the residual smell of urine or poop.
- Set a single area for your dog to do their business. Each time you bring your dog outside to pee or poop, bring them to that same place.
- When you bring your dog out, don't distract them with

a lot of talking or by playing games with them. Establish a routine wherein your dog will learn that you are taking them outside for a single purpose—to do their business.

- Praise your dog when they do their business outside properly. You can also bring treats with you when you take your dog outside to reward them as soon as they are finished. This helps reinforce the behavior of pooping or peeing outdoors.
- Take your dog outdoors regularly to do their business. This is especially true when your dog wakes up in the morning, after each meal, and before going to bed each night.

When it comes to house-training, consistency is extremely important. If you aren't home, make sure that the other members of your household know that they need to take your dog out at regular times throughout the day. When you see that your dog is already getting used to doing their business outside, you can teach them the potty cue.

Basic Obedience Training for Adult Dogs

Basic obedience training involves teaching your dogs the basic commands. These basic commands are called "basic" because they are the easiest to teach dogs, and you can use them when you want to introduce more advanced commands or tricks to your canine companion. Also, basic obedience training makes it easier for you to keep yourself and your dog safe in different kinds of situations.

While you are house-training your dog, you can also start their obedience training. For this, you need a room or space in your home that is free of distractions. Start in such an environment to introduce the commands and practice them a couple of times before moving on to other environments that may contain distractions. Also, make sure that you have enough rewards (like treats or toys) to give your dog one each time they do the command correctly.

When it comes to obedience training, don't expect your dog to learn things in one go. Again, this will depend on a number of factors, such as if your dog has been taught basic commands in the past, the temperament of your dog, the personality of your dog, and even your dog's breed! The simplicity of the command is another factor that will affect the rate at which your dog learns. Here are other pointers for you:

- Maintain consistency throughout your obedience training. This means that you follow the same routine, stick with the same rules, and use the same commands each and every time.
- Dog training is something you will have to do for the rest of your dog's life. And each time you have a training session, make sure to bring a lot of patience with you. This is especially true at the beginning when you are just introducing new commands or tricks.
- Don't give your dog time-outs because they don't understand what these mean. Just correct your dog's behavior right away as soon as you catch them in the act and praise them immediately when they do things correctly.

Basically, to increase the success of your dog's obedience training, make the experience more positive. Set your dog up for success to keep them happy and enthused. This will make your dog training a lot easier and more enjoyable for both yourself and your furry friend.

Adult Dog Training Tips from Experts

Small or big, young or old, dog training is an important part of your dog's life. When you have made the decision to make an adult dog part of your life, keep in mind that you're handling the task of training a dog who has already had a lot of experiences in their life. Therefore, you will be contributing to the lifelong training process that you will continue until your dog grows old. Before you start training, take the time to learn more about your dog in order to understand them better. This will help you determine the best approach to your dog training.

Also, be as realistic as possible when it comes to your dog's training. While it is possible to train adult dogs and teach them new tricks, the process might take more time, effort, and patience than what you expect. No matter how slow your dog's progress is, don't let it discourage you. Invest in your dog, and in time, you will see the fruits of your labor. It's also important to establish a strong bond with your canine. Spend a lot of time with your dog, shower them with affection, and reward them whenever they do something good. These actions will go a long way in motivating your dog. Here are more tips for you from various dog training experts:

- When your dog has already gained mastery of the basic commands, you can move your training sessions to different environments. This will help your canine understand that they should follow you and the commands you give no matter where you are.

- Apart from your training sessions, reinforce the commands you teach by using them throughout the day. For instance, you can ask your dog to "Stay" in preparation for a walk. Or you can ask your dog to "Sit" in the kitchen as you prepare their meal. Using the commands in different situations reinforces them and strengthens the routines you are trying to build.
- Focus on positive reinforcement training methods wherein you use a lot of praise, rewards, and affection while teaching your dog new things. Avoid talking to your dog harshly or using physical abuse as these might have adverse effects on your canine.
- Learn the importance of the basic commands and why you are teaching them. For instance, commands like "Sit" or "Stay" help control the sudden impulses or urges of your dog.
- Instead of expecting your dog to sit, lie down, or calm down all day, help your dog manage their energy. To do this, you must provide your dog with enough mental and physical stimulation to keep them occupied throughout the day. Training is a great way to do this, along with giving your dog toys to play with.

Instead of thinking of dog training as a chore, think of it as spending quality time with your canine companion. Each time you have a training session, this helps enhance your relationship with your dog. As your dog's behavior improves, you will also come to realize that you know them a lot better too. Have fun with training, and it will become a lot easier, both for you and your pet.

Training Adult Dogs to Do New Tricks

It is true that dogs can learn new things no matter what age they are. Some say it's easier to train adult dogs than puppies, while others say the opposite. But you won't really prove this either way unless you have tried training dogs at different ages. Of course, the important thing is the training itself. If you have just brought home an adult dog, training will maintain the sharpness of their mind and provide them with the structure they need to live in the same home as you.

One good thing about adult dogs is that they may have longer attention spans than puppies. They can also adapt quickly to changes in their environment and to new routines compared to puppies. This means that as long as you maintain consistency, you can expect to see the results you desire. For instance, in terms of potty or house-training, adult dogs have more control over their bladder and bowel movements than puppies. And if you have obtained a dog who already has previous house-training experience, then this part of your dog's training will surely be a breeze.

In some cases, you might notice that treats aren't really motivating your adult dog. In such a case, you can focus more on praises and on demonstrating the behaviors for your dog. Then, practice the behavior several times so that your canine starts understanding what you expect of them. Basically, when it comes to adult dogs, you will have to do a lot of observation, reflection, and adjusting to your training plans. Make changes as needed, keep learning more about your dog, and soon, you will discover that your dog is starting to pick up the things you are trying to teach or train them to do!

Chapter 6: Training Senior Dogs

Puppies, young dogs, adult dogs, and now, even senior dogs?

Yes! You can train senior dogs too, whether you have chosen to adopt one or your dog has already grown old and you have now made the choice to train them. As previously mentioned, any dog of any age can be trained. It's never too late. Senior dogs without any formal or structured training still have the ability to understand the concept of obeying commands to get rewards. Even if your senior dog has learned some bad or inappropriate behaviors in the past, you can teach them to think about the behaviors that will earn them a reward and how they should respond when you give specific commands. As with training younger dogs, spending quality time with your senior dog while training them helps strengthen your bond.

As soon as you have brought your older dog home, it's recommended to begin training right away. For this task, the main things you need are patience, time, and treats. Also, before you begin, make sure that you are ready for the task of training a senior dog. For older dogs, reward-based training is one of the most effective methods to use. And if you want to help your senior dog achieve your training goals, use high-value treats to motivate them. Commit to the task, understand the fact that you will be training an older dog, and don't force your canine to do what you want.

If your senior dog grew up with you (but without proper training), you will already know their training history. But if you have decided to adopt a senior dog, then you should speak to your source before you take your dog home. That way, you can find out whether your senior dog has already experienced any kind of training in the past or not. Learning about the training history of your elderly dog is important so that you can come up with a training plan and schedule that your dog can cope with. If your source doesn't know the training history of your dog—such as if you adopt a rescue dog—then you can try to find out for yourself. Try to give your dog the basic commands to see how they will respond. If your dog follows these commands, make a note of the commands they already know. But if your dog just stares at you blankly no matter what command you give, then you may have to start from the very beginning, as you would with puppies or younger dogs.

Since you will be training a senior dog, it's important to consider their health and age while designing your training plans and schedules. Keep in mind that your dog is already old, so they might get tired easily. To make sure that you don't overexert your canine, pay attention to the common signs of exhaustion, such as frequent yawning, excessive licking, drooping ears, ignoring you, and sniffing at the ground.

Should You Train Senior Dogs?

When people adopt senior dogs, or if their dogs have already reached ripe old ages, training them might not be a priority. But even if your dog is already considered a senior, there are many benefits to training them. One of the most important benefits of training senior dogs is that it will give you lots of opportunities to spend time with your aged, fragile canine. If you think that your dog only has a few more years to spend with you, then you should spend as much time as possible with them, right?

Fig. 11: Senior Dog. From Pixabay, by

Also, training your senior dog will help you learn more about them. At several times throughout the day, you will make your dog your main priority as you follow the training session schedules you have set. Throughout the process, you will be able to give your dog a lot of praise, rewards, and love while learning things you never even knew about them. No matter what age dogs are, training helps strengthen the bond between them and their owners. And the stronger this bond is, the more you will love your dog and appreciate them.

The old adage that says that "you can't teach old dogs new tricks" isn't accurate at all. In fact, it's the exact opposite. As long as you keep your training sessions short and use fun, positive ways to motivate your dog, the experience will surely be one your dog will always look forward to. But if you're worried about the health (and age) of your dog, you may consult with a vet first to find out the best training approach to take. It's all about learning what is best for your dog first, then doing everything you can to educate them and help them become better, more well-behaved canine companions.

Things to Remember When Training Senior Dogs

Just because you have an older dog, that doesn't mean that you don't have to train them. Senior dogs are perfectly capable of being trained and of learning new things. In fact, professional dog trainers have seen dogs older than 10 years who perform admirably in training classes. So, if you have a senior dog at home, don't make their age an excuse not to provide them with fun and educational training.

When it comes to "seniority," the age at a which dog qualifies for that classification varies. In general, when small dog breeds reach the age of 12, vets consider them seniors. For bigger dog breeds, vets consider them to be seniors between the ages of 6 and 8. This means that bigger dogs become seniors earlier than smaller dogs, and they have a higher likelihood of showing the most common signs of aging compared to their smaller counterparts. Senior dogs might also show signs of mental aging; however, these are not as noticeable.

Despite all of these aging signs, dogs will always be ready and willing to take part in dog training as long as you find fun, interesting, and motivational methods for the task. Even if your vet advises you to avoid teaching tricks that involve a lot of physical activity, you can still teach simpler commands and tricks to your canine to keep them physically and mentally stimulated. When it comes to training senior dogs, here are some things to keep in mind before you start:

- **It's never too late for treats!**

    Just because you have always believed that old dogs can't learn new tricks, that doesn't mean that you shouldn't try to train your elderly dog. The key to making this easier is to stock up on different kinds of treats! If your dog grew up with you, you should already know what treats they like. If not, then you can experiment with different types of treats to see which one works best for training.

- **Commit to your dog's training by improving your own skills**

    Your dog will only be able to learn as much as you can teach them. No matter how sharp your dog is in their old age, they won't be able to train themselves. Therefore, if you want to make the most out of your senior dog's training, you should learn everything you can about it and try to improve your own skills. The more you practice with your dog, the better you—and your canine—will become.

- **Determine your dog's physical condition and whether it will affect your training**

    If your senior dog is still strong and spritely, then you have nothing to worry about. However, if you notice that your canine already suffers from physical limitations, adjust your training plan accordingly. This is why it's important to consult with your vet first—so you can determine your dog's limitations or if they suffer from any medical condition that you should work around while training.

- **Determine your dog's mental or cognitive abilities and how they might affect your training**

    Sadly, some dogs may develop "Doggie Alzheimer's" when they reach old age. Such a condition will significantly limit your dog's ability to learn new behaviors or tricks. If your dog suffers from this condition, you may notice a number of symptoms, including disorientation, restlessness, decreased hearing, barking aimlessly, losing their ability to recognize their surroundings and the people around them, and losing their previous house-training behaviors.

- **Think about the methods you plan to use for your dog's training**

    We have already gone through the different methods of dog training, and it's up to you as an owner to determine which method is best for your canine. The important thing is to focus on positive methods for training as these will encourage your canine to keep learning with enthusiasm.

- **Try focusing on one task at a time**

    You don't have to feel pressured to "catch up" in terms of dog training. This is especially true if your dog is fairly well-behaved to begin with. While training your dog, try to focus on one task at a time. This helps reduce the confusion, and training won't end up making you—or your dog—frustrated.

- **Think about what you want to teach your dog**

    If you have brought home a dog with a lot of undesirable behaviors, work on helping them unlearn these first. Do this before you try teaching new behaviors. Also, think about your training goals, what you want your dog to achieve after some time. This will help you determine what you want to teach your dog.

- **Make socialization part of your dog's training**

    If you want your dog to feel more open to training, you may consider including socialization as part of your plans. Senior dogs who haven't been trained in the past might not have been exposed to new environments, people, experiences, and animals. Once in a while, take your dog out and expose them to new stimuli to invigorate their mind and motivate them to learn more.

Of course, it goes without saying that you should keep your training sessions short but meaningful. Dog training provides your senior dog with enough challenges to keep their mind sharp and their bodies healthy. Therefore, once you feel like you're ready to take on the task, then it's time to start!

Helpful Tips for Training Senior Dogs

Fig. 12: Training Senior Dogs. From Pixabay, by fernandozhiminaicela, 2018,

Training senior dogs can feel more challenging and time-consuming compared to younger dogs. This is especially true for senior dogs who have had no dog training experiences in the past. But as long as you stick with your training regiment, you will be able to teach your dog the basics to make living with them a lot easier.

When training senior dogs, remember that their brains aren't "primed for learning." This means that they might not be as sharp or as quick to learn as puppies. However, this doesn't mean that your dog is stupid or slow. Think about it; elderly people are still able to learn new things, such as how to use simple technological devices, the names of new people, and so on. Just as senior humans can learn new information and skills, senior dogs have this ability as well. To help improve the chances of your senior dog training's success, here are some tips to keep in mind:

- **Make some modifications to your dog's diet as needed**

    When it comes to your dog's diet, the best person to

talk to about making modifications is a vet. But if you want to ensure the health of your canine as they approach the twilight years, you may want to decrease their protein and fat intake. Also, you can ask your vet about giving dietary supplements to your dog, such as chondroitin and glucosamine. After making any changes, no matter how small, observe your dog carefully to see how these changes affect their health.

- **Keep track of the treats you feed your dog**

    We have already mentioned how reward-based training works well for senior dogs. This means that you will be giving your dogs high-value treats while training. It's important to keep track of how many and how often you give treats to your dog though. That way, you can adjust their diet accordingly to avoid overfeeding.

- **Avoid repetitive physical activities or tasks**

    Keep in mind that senior dogs have older joints—and these don't do well with physical activities that are repeated again and again. This doesn't mean that you shouldn't include any physical tasks or activities in your training. Just make sure that you don't repeat these activities several times without giving your dog a break. This might cause your dog to feel pain, which, in turn, might discourage them from training.

- **Consider the temperature of the environment**

    Senior dogs have a higher sensitivity to extreme temperatures compared to younger ones. Observe your dog for any signs that they are feeling too cold or too hot while training. If you notice any discomfort, take a break and resume your training session when the temperature is more tolerable.

- **Use different kinds of signals while training**

    Apart from verbal commands, try to think of hand signals to pair with them. This helps reinforce your training, thus allowing your dog to learn faster. Hand signals are especially important if your dog is hard of hearing or has already gone deaf. But if your dog has already lost their sense of sight, verbal cues are all you need. Even blind dogs will benefit from dog training, so don't deprive them of it!

- **When your dog is tired, take a break**

    While training, keep an eye on your dog to spot any signs that they are tired, uncomfortable, in pain, or having breathing difficulties. If you observe any of these signs, take a break. Allow your dog to rest where they want to. After some time, you can continue your training session by picking up where you left off.

- **Don't force your dog to do things they aren't able to do**

    Dog training requires a lot of observation and planning. You need to know what your dog is capable of and what they aren't able to do anymore. Plan your training sessions accordingly. If you are trying to teach a command or trick, and your dog doesn't follow you even when you try to entice them with treats, don't force them. Make a note of this behavior and try again next time. If they still refuse, remove it from your plan.

- **As much as possible, have your training sessions in places with soft surfaces**

    This is especially important when you're teaching commands like "Stay," "Sit," "Down," and others that require your dog to get down on the floor. In such cases, prepare a mat or bed for your dog to train on. This will make it easier for your dog to respond or follow your commands, as they will be more comfortable.

- **Include stretches and other gentle exercises in your training routine**

    Gentle exercises such as stretching will help maintain your dog's flexibility, thus allowing them to do more. If needed, speak to your vet about what types of exercises are best for your dog and how much they should exercise each day. That way, you won't end up straining or overexerting your dog.

As you can see, all of these tips focus more on keeping your dog happy and comfortable while training. As with dogs of other ages, it's important to maintain positivity while training to make it worth your dog's while.

Chapter 7: Training Different Dog Breeds

When it comes to learning, does the breed of a dog matter?

This is a very common question posed by dog owners when they consider training their own dogs at home. If you pose this question to dog experts and professional trainers, they might tell you that a dog's breed doesn't matter when it comes to dog training. No matter what breed your dog is, you will be able to train them. Of course, this is true.

But as with other dog parents all over the world, you may be more interested in the level of difficulty when it comes to dog training—and that's why you would be asking the question. While all dogs can be trained, there are certain dog breeds that are considered easier to train and those that are considered difficult to train. But the important thing to keep in mind is that positive reinforcement training methods work for any kind of dog breed, even the more challenging ones. As long as you stick with your dog's training, you're sure to find success.

Dog Breeds and Behaviors

The main reason the ease of dog training may vary between dog breeds is that each breed has its own personality. Think about it; if you have to choose between a sweet-tempered dog breed who loves to learn or a stubborn dog who rarely listens to you, which of these breeds do you think would be more challenging for you to train? And if you're a beginner who doesn't want to be challenged, which breed would you choose?

Knowing that dog breed matters when it comes to the ease of dog training, you should carefully consider what breed of dog you should make a part of your life. Different dog breeds have their own distinctive personalities, which, fortunately, you can observe early on. In terms of personality, dogs can be grouped roughly according to the work they're supposed to do, and this can be a predictor of a dog's temperament when they grow up. Here are some examples of types of dogs and their common personalities:

- **Chasing dogs**

    In general, these dogs are extremely lively, feisty, and active, whether they are puppies or adults. They are also quite fast, which is why they are great at chasing.

- **Guarding dogs**

    These dogs have very strong protective instincts, which is why they are bred for the purpose of guarding flocks. They also have a very strong sense of loyalty.

- **Herding or working dogs**

    These dogs have dispositions that are almost business-like. They have a tendency to think about the situations in front of them before doing their tasks.

- **Hounds**

    These dogs have a tendency to be more independent and aloof. They aren't that interested in socialization with humans, and they have an inclination to do things on their own.

- **Sporting dogs**

    These dogs are adventurous and they love to follow their noses. Also, they always respond enthusiastically when their owners call their names.

These are just some examples of groups of dogs and the possible personalities they may have. Of course, there will always be exceptions to the rule. But more often than not, you can predict the behaviors of your dog based on these groups. It's also important to remember that all dog breeds have their own unique traits, thus making them appealing to different types of people.

Bringing a dog into your life is an important decision to make—and once you make that decision, remember that training your dog is your responsibility. The dog you bring home with you, regardless of breed, will rely on you for their care, health, and welfare. Caring for and training your dog is a lifelong responsibility. Therefore, you should take serious consideration as to whether your lifestyle allows for this kind of responsibility.

After making the decision to bring a dog home, it's time to think about the breed. Since there are some breeds that are easy to train and others that you might find challenging, knowing their breed's general personality can help you out immensely. So, llet's go through some of the most common dog breeds that are easiest and most challenging to train.

The Easiest Dog Breeds to Train

While training a dog is your responsibility as a dog owner, dog training doesn't have to be a difficult thing. Throughout the different chapters of this book, you have already learned a lot of practical and helpful tips for training dogs of all ages. All of this information can help you come up with an effective training plan and schedule to help your canine become healthy, happy, and well-rounded. If you're still thinking about the breed of dog to adopt, you'll be happy to know that there are certain breeds that are easier to train than others. As a beginner, training one of these dogs could potentially make your life a lot easier.

Fig. 13: Border Collie. From Unsplash, by Echo Grid, 2017,

- **Border Collie**

    Whether you already have a lot of dog training experience or this is your first time trying to train a dog, consider adopting a border collie. Dogs of this breed usually come with a lot of energy and always want to please their master. This means that such a dog will always be enthusiastic when it comes to training. However, because of their excessive energy, you should try to match this by coming up with fun, interesting, and stimulating activities for training and do these every day!

- **Border Terrier**

Most dog experts and trainers consider this dog breed to be highly trainable. Border terriers are fairly laid-back, but they do enjoy training and performing different activities. They are affectionate, trainable, and good-tempered too. As with border collies, this dog breed loves pleasing their master. You can use this to your advantage as you shower your dog with a lot of affection to keep them motivated while training.

- **Boxer**

This breed has an even temper and is very intelligen,t making it easy for them to learn new commands. Boxers are active dogs who immensely enjoy mental and physical challenges. They are playful, upbeat, patient, and have a protective nature, making them an excellent breed for families.

- **Doberman Pinscher**

While this dog breed is relatively easy to train, doberman pinschers are recommended for dog owners with more experience. As a beginner, if you are confident that you can provide consistent leadership and training to this dog breed, you can opt to take one home. However, don't let them get lonely or bored as this might cause them to become aggressive or destructive.

- **German Shepherd**

    This breed of dog is always ready to work and eager to please. German shepherds are active, so they need a lot of mental stimulation and physical exercise. They are also well-known for their courage and loyalty. Furthermore, this dog breed also has the ability to learn commands and retain the information they learn for a long time.

- **Golden Retriever**

    In particular, this dog breed makes an excellent companion for those who are new at owning dogs as they love pleasing their masters. Golden retrievers approach life playfully and joyfully, and they maintain this wonderful disposition longer than other dog breeds. One great thing about this dog breed in terms of training is that they learn through trial and error and have a unique ability to solve problems.

- **Labrador Retriever**

    If you're looking for a popular dog breed that's easy to train, then this is the one for you. It's easy to train labrador retrievers whether you want to have one as a working or a family dog. This dog breed also socializes well with humans as well as with other canines. They are non-aggressive by nature, eager to please, and bursting with energy too.

- **Miniature Schnauzer**

    It's easy for this dog breed to learn new tricks and commands. However, this is a very high-energy dog breed that you should keep occupied frequently. Miniature schnauzers crave companionship with humans. Combine this with the intelligence of the breed, and this makes training easy even for beginner dog trainers. This breed is also spunky, alert, and follows commands well.

- **Pembroke Welsh Corgi**

    As another active dog who loves training, this breed loves their human companions and respond to training very well. Apart from training at home, Pembroke Welsh corgis would benefit a lot from enrolling them in obedience classes too. The more you train this dog breed, the more you will see them improve. For the rest of your dog's life, you will enjoy the company of a well-behaved and lovable canine.

- **Poodle**

    Although there are different poodle varieties, all of them are eager to please, incredibly intelligent, and they learn quickly. This dog breed appears on different lists of the easiest dog breeds to handle while training. This is an even-tempered dog that aims to please their masters.

- **Rottweiler**

    This is another dog breed that's easy to train but will keep you busy too. Rottweilers have endurance, intelligence, and a willingness to handle responsibilities. This is why you will see a lot of rottweilers working as therapy dogs, herders, police dogs, and more. Just make sure to socialize this dog breed early on as they have a natural tendency to be territorial.

- **Shetland Sheepdog**

    Finally, this dog breed is very active and performs very well in different kinds of dog sports. Shetland sheepdogs are very easy to train, they're intelligent, and they will always want to please you.

The Most Challenging Dog Breeds to Train

As it is, dog training is already a challenging task, especially for beginners. Challenging but not impossible. While there are dog breeds that are easy to train, there are also those on the opposite side of the spectrum. If you feel intimidated

Fig. 14: Afghan Hound. From Unsplash, by Arve Kern, 2017,

with the task of training a dog and still haven't made a decision about which dog breed to choose, then you should rethink selecting one of these breeds.

- **Afghan Hound**

    While this breed is lovable and faithful, you may experience a lot of challenges when it comes to training, mainly because this breed is extremely independent. Afghan hounds are independent thinkers and tend to be aloof, thus making training quite difficult.

- **American Pit Bull Terrier**

    This breed is considered a fighting dog, and most of them are bred for this exact purpose. But when it comes to training, you might discover that American pit bull terriers aren't that easy to handle. Friendly, loyal, and loving as they are, this dog breed also tends to be very temperamental.

- **Basenji**

    For this dog breed, the first thing you need to do is master crate-training as they tend to be quite stubborn. Basenjis are aloof, independent, and they are too intelligent for their own good. While they may learn the commands and tricks you are trying to teach them, the issue is whether they will perform these commands when asked.

- **Basset Hound**

    What makes this dog breed difficult to train is their notoriously stubborn nature. It's especially difficult if you are a beginner at dog training. In particular, house-training basset hounds is extremely difficult. If you still choose to train this dog (such as if you already have one at home), then you need to have extra patience to stick with training.

- **Beagle**

    As adorable and lovable as this dog breed is, you may experience a lot of frustrations trying to train them. This is because beagles are naturally naughty, thus making training a challenge—even for experienced dog owners.

- **Bulldog**

    This is one dog breed that has become quite popular in recent years. However, as lovable as they are, bulldogs can be very stubborn too. This dog breed may look easy to handle, but they often won't care enough to listen while you are trying to train them.

- **Chihuahua**

    This dog breed is extremely loyal, and they make incredible lapdogs. But they can also be very protective, fierce, and stubborn. As challenging as chihuahuas are to train, this is an essential part of raising this breed, especially in the area of socialization or they might grow up to be aggressive, overprotective, and might end up attacking other people.

- **Chow Chow**

    Raising this dog breed to become well-behaved is an enormous task for any dog owner. Chow chows tend to be stubborn, dominant, and have an unpredictable temperament. They can sometimes be aggressive as well, especially when not trained properly.

- **Pit Bull**

    This dog breed is powerful, strong, and originally bred as fighting dogs. Despite their tough reputation, pit bulls are actually eager to please and very friendly. While they respond well to training, what makes this dog breed difficult is that they get bored very easily. This means that you should stick to a very strict training plan and schedule unless you want your dog to chew, dig, or even become aggressive with other people, dogs, and pets.

- **Pomeranian**

    This fluffy, adorable dog breed comes with a huge personality—and a reputation for being very difficult to train. Without proper socialization early in their life, pomeranians might become either too shy or too aggressive. House-training is also a challenge for this breed because they are very small. Also, this dog breed barks a lot, so training them to be quiet is essential.

- **Pug**

    This dog breed is playful, loyal, smart, and sturdy; however, they can be a challenge to train. Pugs get bored easily, so you need to provide constant stimulation. Also, you need to stick with a very strict training routine to ensure that this dog will achieve the training goals you have set. In particular, this dog breed is very difficult to house-train.

- **Siberian Husky**

    As beautiful as this dog breed is, raising them comes with a lot of challenges. For one, Siberian huskies are extremely active, especially while young. This means that you need to come up with a very dedicated training routine and stick with it. When they get bored, they tend to act out, which means that you should be very consistent when it comes to training them.

General Tips for Training Different Dog Breeds

Dog owners may often end up expecting too much from their canines while training. But when you think about it, expecting your canine to learn basic commands, household rules, and tricks is actually an enormous task. Just as you would teach a baby to crawl, walk, talk, and learn everything they need to survive in the world, training a dog requires a lot of time, patience, effort, and planning. Now that you know that there are breeds that are easier and harder to train, you can take your dog's breed into consideration when planning and scheduling their training. Even though some dogs are harder to train than others, it is entirely possible to train all dog breeds. No matter what breed of dog you own, here are some general tips for you to keep in mind while training:

- **Go slow, especially at the beginning**

    Even before you start training your dog, make sure that

you have prepared an environment where you can train your canine without distractions. Such an environment allows your dog to concentrate fully when you are trying to introduce commands, tricks, and other information. Then, start off with one command at a time. Doing this makes it easier for your dog to learn what they need to and get rewarded for it. The more you reward your canine, the more they will start looking forward to training sessions and to learning new things.

- **Control your dog' training environment**

  Apart from preparing a quiet environment for your dog without distractions, there are other steps you can take to keep your canine focused on the task. Before bringing your dog inside the training environment, make sure that you have picked up any objects that might distract your dog, such as toys, shoes, and such. If you plan to train your dog outdoors, make sure to leash your canine first or use a longline. Also, train your canine within a fenced area.

- **Determine what motivates your dog**

  All dogs are different, and this means that they will be motivated by different things. The great thing about training your dog is that you will learn more about them as time goes by. Over time, you will come to realize what truly motivates your dog and what doesn't. If you want to increase the likelihood of training success, you need to find the rewards that will encourage your dog to continue obeying you and following your commands. This is why it's more recommended to try out different treats and vary the types of treats you give. This keeps your dog interested, and it helps maintain the momentum of your training sessions.

- **Don't just focus on treats all the time**

    When it comes to positive reinforcement, you don't have to use treats alone. There are so many other ways you can repay your canine when they do something right while training. Some examples of non-treat rewards are praise, petting, showing affection, and giving toys. Basically, anything that makes your canine happy would serve as an excellent training reward. If you recall, for a lot of the dog breeds that are challenging to train, one common trait they share is that they love pleasing their owners. So, if you don't think treats are working as effectively as you hoped, then you can try other types of rewards.

- **Be patient**

    This is one tip that has appeared over and over again in the different chapters because it is just so important. No matter what breed of dog you have, no matter what size your dog is, and no matter how old your dog is, patience is essential if you want your training to succeed. Give your dog enough time to learn what you want them to. As long as you are consistent and you keep using positive reinforcement, you're sure to see the results of your training when the right time comes.

- **Tell your dog what you want them to do**

    It's important to remain firm with your dog. There is no

point in teaching your dog a specific set of commands on time then changing those commands after a few months. Once you have created the rules and routine you want your canine to follow, stick with those. Tell your dog exactly what you want them to do and keep practicing until your dog gains mastery. This is the most effective way your dog will learn, and it's also the easiest way for your dog to pick up the things you are teaching them to do.

- **Be careful with how you practice your commands**

   An effective way to reinforce the commands you teach your dogs is practicing those commands as frequently as possible and making them part of your dog's routine. However, you should be careful when practicing those commands. For instance, don't use them only when you want your dog to do something they don't like. If your dog dislikes going into their crate (when you're not yet done with crate-training), don't just use the command "Come" when you want them to go inside their crate. Practice using the command in other ways too. If you only use the command for things your dog doesn't like to do, they might end up disliking the command as well. Mix things up and make sure that you use the commands you teach your dogs both in positive ways and for disciplinary purposes.

- **Make training part of your dog's life**

   We have mentioned how dog training is a lifelong process. Just because your dog has already learned the basic commands plus a few tricks, this doesn't mean that you are done with dog training. Keep in mind that training will provide your canine with the mental and physical stimulation they need to stay healthy. Apart from this, training also gives you an opportunity to bond with your dog each day. While you may reduce the frequency of your dog's training sessions over time, make sure that training becomes a permanent part of your dog's life.

Chapter 8: Common Behavioral Issues in Dogs and How to Deal with Them

Dog training doesn't involve teaching your canine basic commands and tricks only. You can also use it to help "fix" behavioral issues that your dog may have developed or learned throughout their life. Of course, we all want our canines to be well-behaved and happy. This makes it easier for us to live in harmony with each other. As a dog owner, you may experience a number of common behavioral issues at one point or another. In such a case, you must learn how to deal with these issues, and the best way to get rid of them is through training.

Training Hyperactive Dogs to Calm Down

When you have a hyperactive canine, using positive reinforcement training is key. High-energy dogs are very common; however, you shouldn't allow your dog to continue being hyperactive all the time as this will make it very difficult to live with. Also, if left unchecked, a hyperactive dog might learn other destructive behaviors that might be even more difficult to unlearn. If you have a hyperactive dog, here are some tips to help them calm down:

- Manage the excess energy your dog has by making sure that you include a lot of exercise into their daily routine, whether during training or during your free time. Until your dog is fully trained, make sure to leash your dog while doing these physical activities. If you have a fenced yard, you can allow your canine to run around outside for a few minutes throughout the day.
- Another way to help your dog release all that pent-up energy is by taking them to the dog park. This allows your dog to play with other dogs while getting the exercise they need and learning how to interact with other canines.
- Playing games with your canine is an excellent activity too. There are different types of games you can play with your dog both inside and outside of your home. Some great examples of games to play with your canine are:
    - **Find the Treat**

        This is an excellent game to play with dogs who love to explore their environment using their noses. Introduce this game by holding a treat in one hand, tossing it to your other hand, and giving the command, "Find it!" Of course, your dog will find the treat easily. Do this step around 6 to 7 times for your dog to understand the command.

        Then, ask your dog to "Stay" while you walk away from them. Make sure your dog is watching you as you place the treat on the ground. Go back to your dog, pause for a moment, and give the command, "Find it!"

Again, do this step around 6 to 7 times for your dog to understand the command.

Now that your dog understands the game, you can start hiding the treat in different places. Start by hiding the treat in easy-to-find places to give your dog more opportunities to practice. The more you practice, the more difficult locations you can use as your hiding spots.

- **Hide and Seek**

    This is another great game to play with your dog. It's similar to the first game but this time, you would tell your dog to "Find me!" instead of "Find it." Start by hiding in easy locations and giving your dog a treat when they are able to find you.

- Finally, you can also use positive reinforcement training to calm your dog down. The more you use training to calm your dog down, the more they will learn that being too active all the time isn't okay. There are different types of positive reinforcement training methods you can use for this issue, including:
    - Use the command "Sit" as your dog's default behavior. When you feel like your dog is starting to become too energetic, give the command and allow your canine to relax. If your dog is able to sit for an acceptable amount of time, reward them with a treat.
    - If your dog is being hyperactive because they are excited, give the command to "Wait" and ignore your dog until they calm down. Once calm, give a treat and proceed with the activity you were going to do in the first place.

- Use clicker training to help your dog understand that calm behaviors deserve clicks and rewards!

Play Biting, Mouthing, and Nipping

While playfully biting, mouthing, or nipping is normal for dogs, especially puppies, allowing these behaviors to continue into adulthood isn't a good thing. While your puppy might not hurt you when they nip or bite you, these behaviors will become a problem very quickly. If you want to avoid injuries and other issues that might result from these behaviors, here are some tips on how to deal with them:

- Whenever your dog tries to bite, mouth, or nip at you, use a toy as a distraction. Push the toy at the mouth of your dog and try to start a short tug-of-war game. You can give the command "No" when your dog is biting at you, then another command like "Get toy" as you push the toy at their mouth.
- Provide your canine with a wide range of interesting and fun chew toys to keep them distracted. The more toys they have, the less interested your dog will be in biting, mouthing, or nipping at you.
- You can also try to use treats to distract your canine when they start biting, nipping, or mouthing at your hands. Don't use treats too frequently, however, as your dog might learn that these behaviors are good because they get treats after doing them.
- Try not to panic if your dog bites, nips, or mouths at you even after you give them the toy. But if your dog continues the bad behaviors after you gave them the toy, you should stop the behavior. Again, give the

command, "No," this time more firmly, to emphasize that these behaviors aren't okay. If you have to, walk away from your dog so that they learn that when they do these things, you won't play with them.

- If your dog nips at your heels frequently, distract them with a tug toy. Stop moving or walking, then wave the toy in front of your dog's face enticingly. If you aren't carrying a toy, you can simply stop and wait until your dog stops mouthing or nipping at your heels.
- You can also train your dog to perform bite inhibition, the ability to control their mouthing force. Developing this ability in your dog allows them to recognize that the skin of humans is more sensitive. To train your dog to be more gentle, allow them to mouth on your hands. But when your dog bites you hard, give out a yelp immediately, then allow your hand to go limp. This comes as a surprise to your dog, which may cause them to stop. If your dog stops (or if they start licking you), give them a reward, then continue with your game. Repeat these steps 3 times before you take a break. Keep practicing until your dog learns how to be more gentle while playing with you.
- Dogs can also learn bite inhibition by playing with other dogs. In fact, this is where they learn more naturally. Therefore, if you think these behaviors are starting to become a problem, try to increase your dog's social interaction and playtime with other dogs.
- Focus on playing games with your dog that don't involve contact with your hands. This helps satisfy your dog's urge to mouth or bite without hurting you. However, this doesn't mean that you shouldn't play with your dog in general. Play is an important factor that strengthens your bond with your canine. Just choose your games wisely and don't encourage inappropriate behaviors when they happen while you are playing.
- Finally, never use physical punishment, such as hitting

or slapping your dog. This might cause your dog to bite you harder, and it might teach them to become aggressive. As with other issues, focus on positive reinforcement when trying to eliminate these behaviors.

Dealing with Aggression

This is one of the more troublesome issues to deal with. After all, young or old, you wouldn't want to share your home with an aggressive dog, especially if you live with other family members, children, or pets. Aggressive dogs snarl, bare their teeth, pull back their ears, and show other scary behaviors.

Fig. 15: Aggressive Dog. From Pixabay, by Christels

Usually, aggressive canines exhibit such behaviors when they are feeling territorial. If you start with a puppy, then you can discourage aggression early on. Even if you have a dog breed that has a territorial nature, if you shower them with love, affection, and positive reinforcement, you might not have to deal with this issue when they grow up.

However, if you have adopted a young, adult, or senior dog

and discover that they display aggressive behaviors or tendencies, you must work on eliminating these right away. There are many reasons why dogs behave aggressively. To deal with the issue, you should first determine the cause of their aggression. They may react aggressively to something you do, because they are protecting something, because they think you might hurt them, or because they are in pain.

Aggressive dogs are very intimidating, especially when you don't know the reason for their aggression. The key is to remain calm and to never force your dog to do something they obviously don't want to do. It's important to observe your canine carefully, have patience, and approach the situation positively. Here are some tips to help:

- If your dog starts snarling when you get close to them while they are eating, don't approach. This is a natural instinctive reaction. For this, you can casually walk by your dog while they are eating. Don't approach them directly and don't attempt to take away their bowl. Just get your dog used to your presence so that they learn that you aren't a threat even if you stand or walk close to them. You can follow the same approach when your dog is acting aggressively because they are trying to protect something.
- If your dog reacts aggressively when another dog is close, distract them by calling out their name. If your dog looks at you and relaxes, give them a treat. If not, call out their name again while gently tugging on their leash. When rewarding your dog, show enthusiasm so that they know that looking at you instead of at the other dog is a good thing.
- If your dog is acting aggressively because they think you might hurt them, don't force the situation. This may be a common issue for dogs who have been abused in the past. Of course, your canine won't be acting this

way all the time. Whenever your dog is acting calmly toward you, shower them with love, affection, and enthusiasm. Over time, your dog will learn that you aren't a threat.

- You will notice right away if your dog is acting aggressively because they are in pain. Your dog might flinch whenever they move. In such a case, take your dog to the vet and have them checked. The vet can give your dog medications to ease the pain and, hopefully, eliminate the aggressive behaviors too.

When it comes to aggression, the bottom line is to never approach or force a dog who is showing such behaviors. Determine the cause of the behavior, and this will help you come up with a plan to eliminate it.

Chewing, Digging, and Other Destructive Behaviors

Chewing is a natural and normal activity that all canines do. It's also important to help alleviate their anxiety and maintain the health of their teeth. Dogs explore their world through their noses and mouths, and chewing is a method of exploration for them. Unfortunately, allowing your dog to chew everything in sight can be very destructive. To help eliminate this behavior, you can:

- Provide your dog with different kinds of chew toys. Make sure that these are safe, interesting, and fun to chew on.
- Observe your dog as they explore their surroundings. If

they sink their teeth into something they're not supposed to, give the command "No" and replace that item with one of their chew toys.
- Make sure that you don't leave your things lying around the house, especially items that are easy to chew and destroy.

Digging is another destructive behavior that you should help your dog manage. If you have a dog who loves to dig, you should first try to determine the reason for this destructive behavior. If you notice that your dog digs when they are bored, you can play with them more or give them more toys to keep busy throughout the day. In some cases, dogs who are left outside feel vulnerable, and so, they start digging. If you think this is your dog's reason for tearing up your yard, don't leave your canine outdoors for too long. But if your dog is trying to escape, you may need to extend your fence deep into the ground so that they won't be able to. Finally, if you think your dog simply likes digging, it's best to set an area where it's okay for them to dig. Praise your dog for digging in the right spot and reprimand your dog when they dig anywhere else.

There are other types of destructive behaviors that dogs may engage in, and it's important to help your dogs eliminate these behaviors. This process involves training, practice, and consistency. Here are other destructive behaviors that dogs commonly do and how you could get rid of them:

- **Stealing food** is both destructive and dangerous. For this behavior, you should teach your dog some self-control. Do this by teaching the "Wait" command and practicing it in different situations. The "Leave it" command works well here too. After your dog masters these commands, you can go further by teaching your dog what's theirs and what's yours. For this, you can place your food in front of your dog and give a command like "Not for you." If your dog tries to lunge at the food, stop them and repeat the command firmly. If your dog walks away or ignores the food you have placed in front of them, reward them with praise and a treat. Keep practicing this until you notice the behavior disappear.

- **Separation anxiety** is an issue that may cause your dog to start destroying things at home when you leave them alone. You know your dog suffers from this condition when they start becoming very anxious as you prepare to leave. Also, you may start observing the destructive behaviors within 15 minutes after you have left. When you are at home, your dog will constantly follow you and will always try to maintain contact with you as much as possible. To deal with this, you may have to perform behavior modification, desensitization exercises, and a lot of dedicated training sessions. You may want to seek professional help for your dog to overcome this issue.

Barking, Whining, and Other Noisy Behaviors

There's nothing more irritating than a dog who barks non-stop, especially at night. This noisy behavior is common in dogs of different breeds, and it

Fig. 16: Barking Dog. From Pixabay, by dahancoo, 2017. https://pixabay.com/photos/doodle-

can be quite frustrating to help your dog overcome it. But as with other behavioral issues, excessive barking can be eliminated with these proper training techniques:

- If your dog barks non-stop at something, call their name and give the command "Come." This shows that you acknowledge the presence of the thing they are barking at, but you want them to stop barking. If your dog stops barking and comes to you, reward them with a treat.
- If your dog barks at every little thing they see outside, all you have to do is cover up your windows. For most dogs, this solves the barking problem.
- If your dog keeps barking because they are overstimulated, you may try giving them a time out. Do this if the first two tips don't work. Bring your dog to a quiet place and leave them there for some time until they calm down.
- Teach the commands "Quiet" and "Speak" to help your dog learn that there are times when it's appropriate for them to bark and times when they should be quiet. Simply give the command and immediately give a reward when your dog performs the correct action.
- If nothing else works, you may consider using a bark collar (preferably one with a citronella spray, not one that will shock your canine). However, you shouldn't keep this collar on your dog all day—only when they start their barking frenzies.

If your dog whines a lot, the most common reason for this is that they are feeling anxious. Try calming your dog down by showing them some love and affection. Then, you can try the "Quiet" command as you are reassuring your dog. If your dog is whining just to get your attention (for instance, while you are crate-training), ignore the behavior. This will help your dog understand that the behavior won't work as they intend.

Once they stop, reward your dog with a treat. When it comes to noisy behaviors, finding out the cause is essential. Dogs will always have a reason for making noise. Once you discover the reason, you can work on fixing the issue!

Chapter 9: Rewards and Punishments

The choices that dogs make in their lives (and the behaviors that result from these choices) are generally based on whether these choices result in a reward or a punishment. With this in mind, you can say that training involves the manipulation of rewards and punishments in a way that will cause your dog to always make the right choices. If you want dog training to work for you, it's important to learn as much as you can about your dog in order to find out which rewards will truly motivate them.

Back in the 1950s, a man named B. F. Skinner, a behavioral scientist, came up with several principles that apply to any living thing that possesses a central nervous system. One of these principles is that living things have a high likelihood of repeating behaviors that are rewarding to them. Also, they have a low likelihood of repeating behaviors that result in punishment or anything unpleasant. Of course, the application of this principle is quite obvious when it comes to dog training. When you give rewards to your dog for good behaviors, they will most likely repeat them. By contrast, when you punish, ignore, or discipline your dog for doing bad behaviors, they will most likely avoid doing these behaviors again in the future.

Although the definition and explanation of this principle are very clear, when applied to dog training, it isn't that simple. The main reason for this is that punishments and rewards may vary from one dog to another. For instance, one dog may find treats to be highly motivational while another dog prefers affectionate gestures from their owner. On the other side of the spectrum, one dog may learn quickly when you ignore their bad behaviors while another dog may need firmer or stricter methods. To put this in the simplest words, a reward is something your dog likes, and punishment is something your dog doesn't like.

While training dogs, most dog owners use dog treats as rewards. Treats are very effective, as most dogs absolutely love them. When you need to teach tougher commands or tricks, you may opt for high-value treats that are more delectable and appealing to your canine companion. If you have an affectionate dog, you may also use praise, petting, and other affectionate gestures to motivate your dog while training. When it comes to finding the perfect reward, it's up to you as the owner to find out which reward will work best—and you can determine this by learning more about your canine companion.

Punishments, on the other hand, are even trickier. Since positive reinforcement training methods are more recommended than those that involve harsh punishments, how can you punish your canine to teach them to avoid bad behaviors? Well, one effective way to eliminate bad behaviors is to ignore them. Of course, this may not work for all kinds of situations or behaviors. Punishments or discipline should still be part of your dog training though. Later in this chapter, we will go through the most effective ways of disciplining your dog so that you don't have to deviate from positive reinforcement methods of training your furry friend.

Reward-Based Training

When you hear the term reward-based training, your mind probably immediately goes to dog treats, as does ours. When it comes to this type of training, dog treats are the star—and they can be extremely effective for teaching commands and other obedience training concepts. This method of training harnesses the power of a very primal thing—food—and it makes learning easier for dogs too.

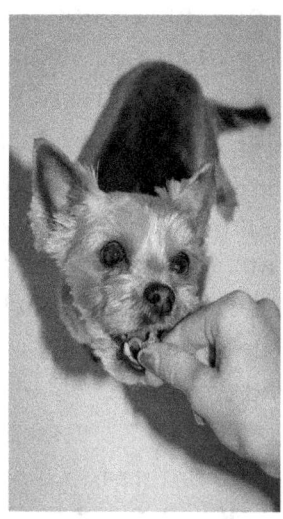

Fig. 17: Treats. From

While most dog owners opt for dog biscuits, these might not work well for all dogs. Some dogs may find these boring, and others might not like the taste. If your dog is a fan of dog biscuits then, by all means, use them! But if your dog isn't interested in these reward, you may have to find other dog treats that will awaken their desire to learn. Sadly, choosing the wrong rewards can have an adverse effect on your training. For instance, if you taught your dog a command, they were able to do it on their first try, and you rewarded them with a treat they don't like, this will decrease the likelihood that your dog will repeat the behavior again in the future.

There is no standard formula for reward-based training. It is a trial and error process wherein you will have to observe your dog to see what they like, what they don't like, and what catches their interest the most. You can come up with a "hierarchy of rewards" for your dog and use this list while training. The more difficult the task is, the higher their reward must be. For instance, if your dog likes biscuits but loves turkey slices, you can use the biscuits to reinforce practices and give turkey slices when you introduce new commands. It's all about matching the reward with the task at hand.

The timing of giving your dog a reward also matters immensely. Right after your dog does something good or right, make sure to give the reward right away. This helps your dog understand that they are getting the reward precisely because they performed the action that you were asking for. When you give the reward even a few seconds after your dog performed the action, they might not understand why they received it in the first place. Timing can either reinforce behaviors or end up confusing your dog. Therefore, you must make sure that your timing is perfect! Here are more tips to keep in mind when it comes to reward-based training:

- The placement of the rewards you give matters too. For instance, if you taught your dog to "Sit," give the treat right after they sit and while they are still in the sitting position. Think about it; if you praise your dog when they sit but give the reward when they stand up, what do you think your dog will learn from this? While timing the reward, make sure your placement is on-point too.
- While training your canine, use light and small treats. These should make your dog feel good, but they shouldn't cause your dog to gain excess weight because you train them frequently. Keep track of the treats you give your dog and adjust their meals as needed.
- Use treats as rewards, not bribes. This means that you should give them after your dog does the command, not before.
- It's best to give your dog a reward when they are in a

calm and submissive state, not when they are hyperactive or excited. Otherwise, you might end up reinforcing the wrong behavior.

- When you are trying to teach your dog a command that involves a lot of steps, you may give them a reward for each step they complete. In such a case, you may use simpler treats for the steps and a high-value treat when your dog reaches the end of the process.

- As you practice commands and behaviors over and over again, try eliminating the use of treats gradually. That way, your dog learns to follow your commands even without treats. When your dog is able to do the commands without the need for treats, you know that they are approaching mastery.

Positive Reinforcement Training

Positive reinforcement training is the easiest and most effective way to train your dog. With this method, you give your dog a reward when they perform good behavior in order to reinforce that behavior. This training method is very powerful, but it's more than just providing praises and rewards. To ensure that you get the most out of this method, you must find the perfect rewards and praise for it. Using these rewards and positive reinforcements will make your training interesting and fun for you and your furry friend. Here are some tips for you to improve your positive reinforcement dog training:

- **Involve everyone in your dog's training**

    This tip applies if you live in a household with other

people, such as the members of your family. After reading this book and learning everything you can about dog training, you can share this information with the other members of your household. That way, they can take charge of training your dog once in a while, especially when you're not around. Involving everyone also means that they take part in reinforcing your training by ensuring that your dog's routine is followed each day, every day. Just make sure that they understand what positive reinforcement means and how to implement it.

- **Vary the rewards you give**

    When it comes to positive reinforcement, treats aren't the only rewards you can give. If you give your dog the same type of reward or the same type of treats over and over again, they will probably get bored. But if you mix things up once in a while and shift between new rewards, rewards your dog really loves, and some "ordinary" rewards, this will keep your dog wanting more.

- **Establish communication with your canine**

    By nature, positive reinforcement methods help you establish communication with your dog. Since you will be giving your canine something positive in return for doing something good, your canine will soon come to understand which behaviors they should do and which aren't appropriate. Make sure to communicate clearly with your canine. And when your dog is doing something that isn't right, be both firm and clear about this as well. This will help give your dog a clearer distinction between what is right and what is wrong.

- **Include games and play in your training sessions**

    Games and play can be fun and effective rewards for your canine. But don't use them in the middle of your training session as this might leave your dog confused. Instead, when your training session is coming to an end, you can ask your dog to do something you know they're already familiar with. When your dog performs the action correctly, you can start a game or initiate play as their reward. That way, you can extend the bonding time you have with your dog, end the training session on a positive note, and make your dog appreciate you more.

- **Also, include outdoor activities in your training sessions**

    Dogs love going outside! So, once in a while, you can make your training sessions even more fun by having them outside. Of course, you should only do this when you are reinforcing concepts or commands that you have already introduced. However, it's not a good idea to train your dog outside when you are trying to introduce new concepts, commands, or information to your canine. With all the new stimuli in the great outdoors, your dog will have a very hard time focusing on you.

- **Make your training sessions short, sweet, and simple**

    This is especially important at the beginning of your

training. When making your training sessions, don't try to have sessions that are half an hour long or more. Remember that dogs have shorter attention spans than us humans. Also, don't plan training sessions in which you will teach your dog 4 or more commands or tricks at a time. If you want to get the most out of each training session, keep them short, limit the information, and provide a lot of positive reinforcement.

- **Always correct your dog as needed**

    Finally, although positive reinforcement training focuses more on reinforcement, you shouldn't be afraid to correct your dog as needed. Yes, you should encourage and reinforce their behaviors using positive methods. But if your dog is doing something bad, dangerous, or inappropriate, you should correct the behavior too. Just make a clear distinction between your reinforcements and your corrections to ensure that your dog only learns the right things.

Should Punishments Be Part of Your Training?

In terms of dog training, punishment refers to something that happens around or to a dog that reduces the likelihood that they will repeat the behavior that preceded it. Punishment can come in the form of deliberate things, such as a stern warning, a physical hit, or something else. It can also come in the form of accidental things, including stepping on something sharp, or coming into contact with something hot. No matter what, as long as the dog experiences something painful or unpleasant, this can be considered as punishment.

Now that you know this definition of punishments in the context of dog training, should you include them as part of your training?

That depends.

Physical punishment such as hitting, beating, or spanking your dog has no place in positive reinforcement training. These are considered aversive techniques wherein a dog feels pain where they are hit. While using physical punishment may eliminate bad behaviors, this might also cause other adverse effects on your dog. For one, your dog might learn to become aggressive if you always hit them. Some dogs become fearful of their owners too. Also, when you hit your dog, you can forget about forming a strong and loving bond with them. Most likely, your dog will see you as nothing more than an authority figure they must obey unless they want to get hurt. Apart from the pain they feel, physical punishment may also increase the dog's stress significantly while lowering their quality of life. Why do this when there are better ways?

There is such a thing as "positive punishment" in which you would do something around or to your dog that they don't like. This is considered "positive" because it doesn't involve harshness and pain; you are simply "adding" something to the environment of your dog that they don't like. These things are called "aversives," and they come in different forms. Some of the more common aversives are rattle bottles, heeling sticks, spray collars, and so on. You may consider using these in your training as an alternative to negative punishment, which may harm your dog in different ways.

Effective Ways to Discipline Your Dog

Disciplining your dog is part of the training process. Without discipline, you might just end up with a spoiled adult dog who does whatever they want, whenever they want. And you don't want to have a dog like that. Although punishment is usually seen as a bad thing, it doesn't always have to be. Disciplining your dog by incorporating punishments will help your canine understand what they are allowed to do and what they aren't allowed to do. There are simple kinds of punishments that you can carry out that are both efficient and humane. Some examples of these are:

Fig. 18: Dog

- Taking your dog's toys away.
- Using a firm tone to stop your dog's behavior and pairing this with an equally firm restraining action.
- Ignoring your dog until they stop the behavior.

As you can see, these punishments give a clear message, but they won't make your dog feel wary, fearful, or angry at you. Consistently giving these punishments will help your dog see and understand that you won't tolerate the behavior they just did. When it comes to giving punishments while training, here are some things to keep in mind:

- When thinking of a punishment to give your dog, make sure that it matches the severity of the misbehavior for it to stick. For instance, if your dog is simply acting too excited, your punishment can be to ignore them. But if your dog is doing something dangerous or inappropriate, you should think of a more urgent and firm punishment to let your dog know that what they are doing isn't okay.
- Just as you give rewards, make sure to give your punishment immediately after your dog's behavior. This will help your dog understand that the behavior that you are punishing is the one they have just done.
- When dealing with an aggressive dog, be very careful in giving punishments. Never approach such a situation with heightened emotions. For instance, if your dog is growling at you or a member of your family, never lunge at your dog while giving a stern command. This might surprise your canine, causing them to lunge back at you or even bite you. Instead, remain calm while you are giving your stern command. Once your dog calms down, you can give them a treat and shower them with affection. Of course, you should also learn the cause of your dog's aggression so that you can help avoid the behavior entirely.
- Finally, after punishing your dog, make sure to teach a good behavior in replacement of the bad one. Distracting your dog by teaching them a good behavior may help your dog forget the bad behavior more easily. Doing this teaches your dog how to behave when faced with a specific situation. In some cases, when you don't teach a new behavior, your dog becomes confused. And when the same situation arises, your dog might just go back doing the behavior you punished them for.

Dog discipline involves training your dog to differentiate

acceptable behaviors from unacceptable ones. Using positive punishment or disciplinary techniques is a lot more effective than trying to strike fear into your dog by hitting them or being very harsh with them. Here are a few more effective tips to help you discipline your dog without using harsh punishments:

- First, keep in mind that your dog's behavior isn't malicious or purposely done. More often than not, dogs are just bored, or they do things because these behaviors seem "normal" to them. If you catch your dog doing something wrong, it's up to you to educate them.
- You may want to think of a correcting cue to say when your dog is doing something wrong. The common ones are "No," "Think again," "Stop," and "Leave it," each of which convey a clear meaning. Train your dog to learn the meaning of this word or phrase by saying it each time your dog does something bad, then rewarding them if they stop.
- Try doing the "scruff-shake." For this, grab hold of the fur under your dog's neck or ears and give them a brisk but brief shake. Do this when you catch your dog in the act of doing something bad. This action comes as a surprise to your dog, thus stopping the behavior immediately.
- Also, try doing the "put-down" move. To do this, push your dog over gently but quickly onto their back or side then lean over them. This shows your dog that you're dominant, and they must follow you.
- Time-outs work well too, and you can do them in different ways. You can ignore your dog, stop interacting with them, stop playing with them, or place them in an isolated place for a couple of minutes. Do this right after you catch them doing something bad.

When it comes to doggy discipline and giving punishments,

the key is to find the perfect balance between helping your dog learn that the behavior they are doing is unacceptable and considering your dog's feelings. You shouldn't be too strict nor should you be too much of a pushover. Remember, you are only doing this for the good of your dog. So, stick with your disciplinary methods to ensure that your canine will learn what's right and what's not.

Chapter 10: Advanced Training Tips and Tricks

Dog training is truly important. It's something that no dog owner should ever ignore! A lot of dog owners out there may feel complacent as long as their dogs aren't aggressive or don't misbehave all the time. But even if your dog is fairly well-behaved without training, you should still engage in dog training—and now you know why. Unless you are aiming to teach your dog complicated tricks or train them to do a specific task, dog training doesn't have to be that difficult. As long as you can teach your dog the basic commands and a few simple tricks, living with your dog will be a whole lot easier. Plus, you and your canine will be able to enjoy all the benefits dog training has to offer.

Once you have made the commitment to include dog training into your dog's daily life, you may soon discover how much fun this challenge is. The closer you get to your dog, the more you learn about them. And the more you see how your dog improves and progresses, the more motivated you may become to push yourself and your canine

Fig. 19: Precision Training. From Pixabay, by MabelAmber, 2018.

companion even further! If you have finished all the basics and want to encourage your dog to learn more, this chapter will be a huge help. As long as you make dog training a positive thing, your dog will surely love every minute of it. And since dog training is a lifelong process, learning these advanced tips, tricks, and strategies will help you out a lot.

Precision Dog Training

Have you ever heard of precision dog training? This is a more advanced type of dog training wherein you go beyond the basics to make sure that you always have your dog under control no matter what the situation may be. Although you may have no plans to have your dog compete in shows, precision dog training is something you can do to enrich your dog's life and improve their behaviors.

By the name itself, you should know that this type of dog training is more strict and more precise. Only the most dedicated dog owners take their dog's training further than the basic commands. If you're one such dog owner, then you can also give precision dog training a try. After you have finished this basic training and are confident with the commands and skills your dog has learned, then you can move on to the more advanced stuff. Never rush basic training as this will be the foundation of other types of training you plan to do in the future. Therefore, you can only consider doing precision training and other advanced training methods when you have observed that your dog shows consistency in terms of following basic commands along with the routine and rules you have set.

As a dog owner, it is your choice whether you want to continue your dog's training or not. While this is highly recommended, it's understandable for some people to just stick with the basics. There is nothing wrong with this, of course, as long as you maintain your dog's training throughout their life. But if you're interested in precision dog training, some of the most common things to teach your dog are:

1. **Off-Leash Training**

    While your dog follows all of your commands when you are in familiar environments or while your dog is on a leash, don't expect the same once you remove the leash and your dog realizes that they are free. Obviously, the difference between off-leash training and basic training is that the former doesn't involve a leash. For this type of training, you will re-train your dog with the basic commands and other tricks, only this time, you won't use a leash. As with basic training, start slow.

    Don't attempt to train your dog off-leash for the first time in a dog park or other equally busy environment. Start in distraction-free, enclosed environments, allowing your dog to explore without their leash. Then, teach the basic commands and keep practicing them each day. For this type of training, the most important command to help your dog master is "Come." That way, no matter how big the environment is or how far your dog goes, they will surely return to you when you give this command.

2. **Using Hand Signals**

    Another way to enhance your training and reinforce the commands you teach your dog is by teaching hand signals. This is especially beneficial if your dog's hearing starts to weaken as they age. Hand signals are also very effective when you are training your dog off-leash and from a distance. Hand signals are your secondary way to communicate with your dog.

The choice of what signals to use is up to you. As long as your dog can differentiate between the signals you come up with, you don't have to worry. You can use the same signals as those used by professional dog trainers or you can come up with your own unique signals to indicate the commands. Keep practicing these signals both on and off-leash until your canine understands that they mean.

Tips for Training Working Dogs

Working or service dogs help people in their daily lives so that they don't have to depend heavily on others. In some cases, owners may want to train their dogs to help out at home and serve as working dogs even though they haven't been professionally trained. In the simplest terms, working dogs are trained to take specific actions as needed in order to help their masters. The dog is able to perform tasks according to what you have trained them to do.

Working dogs aren't required to be trained by professionals. This means that you can also train your dog at home according to your own needs and the tasks you want them to do. Before training, make sure that your dog meets shows the following characteristics:

- Is willing to please you
- Can reliably perform tasks over and over again
- Is able to remain calm no matter what surroundings they are in
- Is able to socialize in different environments and situations
- Has the ability to learn information and retain what they have learned
- Remains alert, though not reactive

If you want your dog to become a working dog, help them master the basics first, including house-training, socialization, and the basic commands. Also, make sure that your dog learns to focus solely on you no matter how many distractions there are in the environment. Then, you can start thinking about what tasks you want your dog to learn. Upon determining these tasks, you can start training your dog to take a specific action when you need assistance. To help you with training, here are some tips to keep in mind:

- Start your dog's task-specific training as early as possible.
- Build a genuine and loving relationship with your dog.
- Make sure that your dog is at the peak of health and receiving enough exercise time to remain strong.
- Groom and handle your dog with care each day.
- Enrich your dog's mental health by providing a lot of activities that involve nose work, mind puzzles, playtime, and socialization.
- Help your dog master obedience training before transforming them into a working dog.
- Allow your dog to have some fun too.

As with other types of dog training, this takes time. If you want to have a working dog, put in the time and effort to train them. Also, keep practicing the basics once in a while so that your dog never forgets them.

Training Small Dogs

Most of the time, smaller dogs are able to do things that big dogs aren't allowed to do, and this is mainly because of their diminutive sizes. However, this doesn't mean that if you have a small dog, you should allow them to do whatever they want at home. While you would use the same basic principles and techniques for training bigger dogs, there are some size-specific tips you may want to use to ensure that your tiny dog's training goes smoothly. Here they are:

- **Go down to your dog's level**

    Because of their size, small dogs may feel intimidated or threatened by how big you are. Instead of looming over your dog, go down to their level. This helps prevent your dog from becoming unresponsive, intimidated, or defensive while you are training.

- **Help your dog master the basic commands to ensure their safety**

    To ensure the safety of your small dog, the first commands you should teach them are "Sit," "Stay," and "Down." These will help your dog become more well-behaved, and they will also help prevent your canine from darting away from you, especially in unsafe environments.

- **Make sure your dog knows who is in charge**

    A lot of small dogs tend to feel like they are the rulers in their homes. If you allow this thinking to continue, you'll end up having a little diva who doesn't listen to you. From the get-go, make sure that your dog knows who is in charge—and that's you! Do this by remaining firm with your dog, especially when they are doing inappropriate or wrong things. The more your dog realizes that they can't get away with everything, the more they will come to respect you and see you as their master.

- **Try different training methods to see what works**

    Just because you have a small dog doesn't mean that they cannot learn as much as big dogs. As with any other type and size of dog, treat your miniature one as a blank slate. Try different things to see what works, what your dog excels at, and what you may need to change in your training plans.

Training Large Dogs

If personality is a big issue for smaller dogs, handling is the main issue for large ones. Imagine having to calm down an enormous dog when they are excited about something! When it comes to large dogs, obedience training becomes even more important as the risks that come with misbehaving increases significantly as the size of the dog increases. Training is essential to ensure your safety, your dog's safety, and the safety of those around you. Here are some tips to keep in mind when training large dogs:

- **Start off with basic commands to help you control your dog**

    As with small dogs, there are basic commands that you may want to teach first in order to make it easier to live with, manage, and train. These basic commands include "Heel" (learning to walk on a leash), "Down" (not jumping up at you), and "Get off" (not climbing on the furniture).

- **Make eye contact as you give commands in a firm way**

    Performing these two actions while training your dog helps them learn that you are serious about your commands and will not back down. While maintaining eye contact, give your commands in a clear and loud voice. This will make an impression on your dog, even with their intimidating size.

- **While training your dog, make sure that there aren't any children or animals in the room**

    Training large dogs in quiet and calm environments is the way to go. Otherwise, your large dog will get distracted or excited with the presence of children, other dogs, or other types of pets. Also, keeping them away helps ensure their safety while your dog hasn't mastered their training yet.

More Advanced Training Tips and Tricks

When it comes to dog training, the possibilities are endless. There will always be more things to teach your dog. But this doesn't mean that you should rush your training sessions just that so you can continue teaching your dog more and more things. Remember that this is something you will be doing throughout your dog's life. So, take things slow, give your dog time to master commands and tricks, and keep these final tips in mind:

Fig. 20: Dog Tricks. From Pixabay, by Katrin B,

- **If you notice that your dog has excess energy, use training to help burn this energy off**

    Allowing your dog to burn their excess energy in productive ways will help you avoid a lot of issues. Often, dogs who have too much energy end up being noisy, destructive, and frustrating. You can't blame your dog as they aren't in control of how much energy they have. Instead, help your dog overcome this by allowing them to get a lot of exercise throughout the day. Use training and playtime to accomplish this.

- **Set clear rules and boundaries for your dog**

  Do this from the very beginning. Set clear rules and boundaries, then introduce these to your dog one at a time through training. If you see that your dog has forgotten any of these rules, correct them. If you have to, re-train your dog so that they will learn these things again. When your dog knows the rules and boundaries, you can enjoy a harmonious relationship with them.

- **Don't give your dog the same treatment as human beings**

  Dogs aren't people, no matter how human-like they may seem. Therefore, you shouldn't treat your dog like a human nor should you expect them to respond like a human. This is why you should learn how to communicate in a way your dog will understand—by using clear, simple commands, hand signals, and body language.

- **Avoid scolding your dog**

  No matter how many mistakes your dog makes throughout your training, keep in mind that they are doing their best. Never forget that dogs learn at different rates. If your dog takes a long time to learn a certain command, don't scold them for it. This type of punishment makes dog training a negative experience instead of a positive one.

Conclusion: Training Your Dog the Right Way

There you have it... everything you need to know about dog training. Whether you want to teach your dog the basic commands, potty-training, or other advanced tasks, you are now armed with the knowledge to do so. While the concepts involved in dog training are simple, the actual process is a long and tedious one. But as long as you remain patient, consistent, and committed to your dog's training, you will surely succeed.

Fig. 21: Strong Bond. From Unsplash, by Humphrey Muleba, 2018,

From puppies to young dogs to adult dogs to senior dogs, you have learned how to approach training the right way. You have even learned which dog breeds are easy and difficult to train. This information is particularly useful if you are still trying to determine which dog breed to get. No matter what dog breed or stage of life your dog is in, it all boils down to communicating with your dog properly. Training is all about communication and finding out how your dog learns. While employing the different tips you have learned here, if you find that something doesn't work, change it! If you find that some of the techniques work effectively with your dog, then keep doing them.

As the trainer, you should be able to gauge how well your dog training is going. Don't expect your dog to tell you what's working and what isn't. Nor should you expect your dog to tell you what they like and what they don't. It's up to you as the owner to observe your canine and determine what can help improve and enrich your training sessions. Now that you have learned all the fundamental information to train your dog, it's time to start applying it. There's no time like the present to start your dog training journey. So, go ahead and begin strengthening your bond with your furry companion and teach them how to truly become man's best friend!

References

5 Cool Tricks to Teach Your Dog. (2019). Retrieved from https://www.purina.co.uk/dogs/key-life-stages/puppies/cool-dog-tricks-advanced-training

5 Dog Training Tips for a Great Family Dog. (2019). Retrieved from https://www.bupa.com.au/pet-insurance/dog-training-tips-family-dog/

5 Essential Commands You Can Teach Your Dog. (2018). Retrieved from https://www.cesarsway.com/5-essential-commands-you-can-teach-your-dog/

7 ways to discipline your dog. (2019). Retrieved from http://www.humansfordogs.com/2009/11/7-ways-to-discipline-your-dog.html

10 Advanced Security Training Tips for Personal Protection Dogs. (2019). Retrieved from https://www.expertsecuritytips.com/advanced-training-tips-for-dogs/

10 Best Training Tips. (2019). Retrieved from https://www.pedigree.com/dog-care/training/10-best-training-tips

10 Small Dog Training Tips. (2019). Retrieved from http://www.animalplanet.com/pets/top-10-tips-for-training-your-small-dog/

Adult and Senior Dog Training. (2019). Retrieved from https://www.purina.co.uk/dogs/behaviour-and-training/training-your-dog/ongoing-training-for-your-dog

Adult Dog Training – 10 Professional Trainer Tips. (2019). Retrieved from https://servicedogacademy.com/wp/free-dog-training-advice/adult-dog-training-10-professional-trainer-tips/

Advanced Dog Training. (2019). Retrieved from https://www.precision-dog-training.com/advanced-dog-training.html

Baker, L. How to Train Big Dogs. (2019). Retrieved from https://m.wikihow.com/Train-Big-Dogs

Basic Dog Obedience Training For Your Family Pet. (2019). Retrieved from https://www.precision-dog-training.com/basic-dog-obedience-training.html

Basic Dog Training Commands. (2019). Retrieved from https://www.purina.co.uk/dogs/behaviour-and-training/training-your-dog/basic-commands-for-your-dog

Basic Obedience Training for Dogs. (2019). Retrieved from https://www.instructables.com/id/Basic-Obedience-Training-for-Dogs/

Becker, M. 7 Tips for Training a Stubborn Dog. (2015). Retrieved from http://www.vetstreet.com/our-pet-experts/7-strategies-for-training-a-stubborn-dog

Becker, M. Dog Training 101: Essential Tools You'll Need. (2017). Retrieved from http://www.vetstreet.com/our-pet-experts/dog-training-101-essential-tools-youll-need

Becker, M. Your Dog Is Never Too Old for Training. (2012). Retrieved from http://www.vetstreet.com/our-pet-experts/your-dog-is-never-too-old-for-training

Bender, A. Teach an Old Dog New Tricks: 5 Training Tips. (2019). Retrieved from https://www.thesprucepets.com/training-tips-for-adult-dogs-1118253

Bender, A. Top 5 Ways to Use Positive Reinforcement to Reward a Dog. (2019). Retrieved from https://www.thesprucepets.com/ways-to-reward-a-dog-1118276

Bender, A. Training Small Dogs: What You Need to Know. (2019). Retrieved from https://www.thesprucepets.com/tips-for-training-small-dog-breeds-1118254

Bender, A. Why Positive Reinforcement Dog Training Works. (2019). Retrieved from https://www.thesprucepets.com/positive-reinforcement-dog-training-1118248

Berman, N. The 20 Most Difficult Dog Breeds to Train. (2017). Retrieved from https://puppytoob.com/20-difficult-dog-breeds-train/

Bolluyt, J. These Are the Dog Breeds That Are Notoriously Difficult to Train. (2018). Retrieved from https://www.cheatsheet.com/culture/dog-breeds-that-are-difficult-to-train.html/

Bolluyt, J. 18 of the Easiest Dog Breeds to Train. (2018). Retrieved from https://www.cheatsheet.com/culture/easiest-dog-breeds-to-train.html/

Bourne, S. How to Handle 6 Common Dog Behavior Problems. (2019). Retrieved from https://www.petcarerx.com/article/how-to-handle-6-common-dog-behavior-problems/1461

Can you teach an old dog new tricks: Here's how! (2019). Retrieved from https://tractive.com/blog/en/training-en/can-you-teach-an-old-dog-new-tricks-check-tips

Clark, M. How Much Training Is Too Much Training For Your Dog? (2019). Retrieved from https://dogtime.com/reference/dog-training/50681-much-training-much-training-dog

Clark, M. 7 Most Popular Dog Training Methods. (2019). Retrieved from https://dogtime.com/reference/dog-training/50743-7-popular-dog-training-methods

Cole, L. 6 Benefits of Obedience Training for Dogs. (2017). Retrieved from https://www.canidae.com/blog/2017/09/6-benefits-of-obedience-training-for-dogs/

Coren, S. Dogs Learn by Modeling the Behavior of Other Dogs. (2013). Retrieved from https://www.psychologytoday.com/us/blog/canine-corner/201301/dogs-learn-modeling-the-behavior-other-dogs

Day, L. 5 Steps to Create Your Puppy Training Schedule. (2019). Retrieved from https://pupbox.com/training/puppy-training-schedule/

Different Kinds Of Dog Training. (2015). Retrieved from https://www.cesarsway.com/different-kinds-of-dog-training/

Dog - Breed-specific behaviour. (2019). Retrieved from https://www.britannica.com/animal/dog/Breed-specific-behaviour

Dog Discipline – Should We Beat or Hit a Dog as Punishment? (2019). Retrieved from https://shibashake.com/dog/dog-discipline-punishment-beat-hit-dog

Dog Discipline: Does Hitting and Beating a Dog Work? (2019). Retrieved from https://pethelpful.com/dogs/An-Ear-for-an-Ear-Why-Biting-your-Dogs-Ear-Does-not-Work-aversive-techniques-forceful-punishment-do-not-work

Dog Training FAQ's. (2019). Retrieved from http://petkey.org/dog-training/trainingfaqs.aspx

Duno, S. Are You Making These 10 Training Mistakes? (2019). Retrieved from https://moderndogmagazine.com/articles/are-you-making-these-10-training-mistakes/29092

Easter, F. Do Different Dog Breeds Learn Differently? (2018). Retrieved from https://www.animalbehaviorcollege.com/blog/do-different-dog-breeds-learn-differently/

Effects of Dog Breed on Dog Training Effectiveness. (2014). Retrieved from https://unleashedjoy.com/breeds-harder-train-others

Elliott, P. How to Punish a Dog. (2019). Retrieved from https://www.wikihow.com/Punish-a-Dog

Elliott, P. How to Train an Adult Dog. (2019). Retrieved from https://www.wikihow.com/Train-an-Adult-Dog

Erb, H. Dog Training Tips: How to Train a Dog. (2017). Retrieved from https://www.akc.org/expert-advice/training/12-useful-dog-training-tips/

Fallis, C. Training a Senior Dog — And Other Valuable Advice. (2013). Retrieved from https://www.petful.com/behaviors/training-a-senior-dog/

Finlay, K. 12 Of The Easiest Dog Breeds To Train. (2019). Retrieved from https://iheartdogs.com/easiest-dog-breeds-to-train/

Freitag, S. 7 Reasons You Should Train Your Dog. (2016). Retrieved from https://www.theodysseyonline.com/7-reasons-you-should-train-your-dog

Gabbard, J. 10 Tips That Make Dog Training Easier. (2019). Retrieved from https://www.puppyleaks.com/dog-training-easier/

Geier, E. The 7 Basic Must-Haves for Training Your Dog. (2019). Retrieved from https://www.rover.com/blog/basic-must-have-items-dog-training-in/

Get Started in Dog Training: Tips & Techniques for Beginners. (2019). Retrieved from https://www.thekennelclub.org.uk/training/get-started-in-dog-training/

Gibeault, S. Positive Rewards Dog Training Tips. (2018). Retrieved from https://www.akc.org/expert-advice/training/training-rewards/

Gibeault, S. The Importance of Training Your Senior Dog. (2017). Retrieved from https://www.akc.org/expert-advice/training/training-your-senior-dog/

Gigler, J. 5 Essential Dog Training Supplies. (2019). Retrieved from https://www.whole-dog-journal.com/training/5-essential-dog-training-supplies/

Harleman, J. How to Teach Your Old Dog New Tricks. (2019). Retrieved from https://www.rover.com/blog/teach-old-dog-new-tricks/

Heimbuch, J. 11 tricks you can teach a senior dog. (2015). Retrieved from https://www.mnn.com/family/pets/stories/11-tricks-you-can-teach-senior-dog

Helderman, J. 10 Bad Things That Happen When You Baby Your Dog. (2016). Retrieved from https://www.countryliving.com/life/kids-pets/g3433/bad-things-that-happen-when-you-spoil-your-dog/

Horwitz, D. Puppy Behavior and Training - Training Basics. (2019). Retrieved from https://vcahospitals.com/know-your-pet/puppy-behavior-and-training-training-basics

House Training Adult Dogs. (2019). Retrieved from https://pets.webmd.com/dogs/guide/house-training-adult-dogs#1

Housetraining Adult Dogs: Training Tips And Techniques. (2019). Retrieved from https://dogtime.com/dog-health/general/360-housetraining-for-adults

House Training Your Puppy. (2019). Retrieved from https://pets.webmd.com/dogs/guide/house-training-your-puppy#1

How To Create A Puppy Schedule. (2015). Retrieved from https://www.cesarsway.com/how-to-create-a-puppy-schedule/

How to Potty Train a Puppy: Tips for New Pet Parents. (2019). Retrieved from https://www.petco.com/content/petco/PetcoStore/en_US/pet-services/resource-center/behavior-training/Tips-and-Tricks-for-Housetraining-a-Puppy-or-Dog.html

How To Train A Dog The Right Way. (2019). Retrieved from https://www.dog-training-excellence.com/how-to-train-a-dog.html

How to Train Your Dog & Top Training Tips. (2019). Retrieved from https://www.rspca.org.uk/adviceandwelfare/pets/dogs/training

Is it important to train my dog? What sort of training would you recommend? (2019). Retrieved from https://kb.rspca.org.au/knowledge-base/is-it-important-to-train-my-dog-what-sort-of-training-would-you-recommend/

Karetnick, J. Service Dogs 101: Everything You Need To Know About Service Dogs. (2019). Retrieved from https://www.akc.org/expert-advice/training/service-dogs-101/

Kaschel, R. Are Some Breeds Harder to Train Than Others?

(2019). Retrieved from https://www.petsafe.net/learn/are-some-breeds-harder-to-train-than-others

King, A. Training Tips: Can You Teach An Old Dog New Tricks? (2016). Retrieved from https://www.wideopenpets.com/can-you-teach-an-old-dog-new-tricks/

Kuras, A. 15 Helpful Dog Training Tips From The Experts. (2015). Retrieved from https://www.care.com/c/stories/6540/15-helpful-dog-training-tips-from-the-experts/

Lissa, S. 10 Common Dog Behavior Problems And How To Solve Them. (2019). Retrieved from https://www.dogviously.com/dog-behavior-problems/

Lotz, K. Top 10 Senior Dog Training Tips. (2019). Retrieved from https://iheartdogs.com/top-10-senior-dog-training-tips/

Lunchick, P. 5 Simple Commands You Should Teach Your Puppy. (2018). Retrieved from https://www.akc.org/expert-advice/training/teach-your-puppy-these-5-basic-commands/

Mattinson, P. Punishment In Dog Training. (2015). Retrieved from https://thehappypuppysite.com/punishment-in-dog-training/

McMahan, D. What your dog's bad behavior says about you. (2017). Retrieved from https://www.nbcnews.com/better/health/what-your-dog-s-bad-behavior-says-about-you-ncna795666

Meyers, H. Puppy Potty Training Schedule: A Timeline For Housebreaking Your Puppy. (2019). Retrieved from https://www.akc.org/expert-advice/training/potty-training-your-puppy-timeline-and-tips/

Millan, C. Starting Your Puppy Off Right! (2015). Retrieved from https://www.cesarsway.com/starting-your-puppy-off-right/

Miller, P. Training a Hyperactive Dog to Calm Down. (2019). Retrieved from https://www.whole-dog-journal.com/behavior/training-a-hyperactive-dog-to-calm-down/

Miller, P. Training An Older Dog - Whole Dog Journal. (2019). Retrieved from https://www.whole-dog-journal.com/training/training-an-older-dog/

Miller, P. Understanding Reward Based Dog Training. (2019). Retrieved from https://www.whole-dog-journal.com/training/understanding-reward-based-dog-training/

Miller, P. Young Dogs Learn From Older Well-Behaved Dogs. (2019). Retrieved from https://www.whole-dog-journal.com/training/young-dogs-learn-from-older-well-behaved-dogs/

Mouthing, Nipping and Play Biting in Adult Dogs. (2019). Retrieved from https://www.aspca.org/pet-care/dog-care/common-dog-behavior-issues/mouthing-nipping-and-play-biting-adult-dogs

New Tricks: Dog Training Tips For Puppy, Adult, & Senior Dogs. (2019). Retrieved from https://www.justrightpetfood.com/blog/dog-training-tips-for-puppy-adult-senior-dogs

Obedience Training for Dogs. (2019). Retrieved from https://pets.webmd.com/dogs/guide/dog-training-obedience-training-for-dogs#1

Ohlms, S. 7 tips for training your dog, from a Marine who trained dogs to sniff out bombs. (2019). Retrieved from https://www.businessinsider.com/7-tips-for-training-your-dog-from-a-military-dog-handler-2019-5#7-not-every-dog-is-going-to-be-able-to-learn-every-task-7

Parks, S. The First 5 Things to Teach Your New Puppy (and When to Start). (2019). Retrieved from https://www.rover.com/blog/can-train-puppy-first-day-heres/

Pennings, S. Precision K9 Dog Training - Obedience for the Family Dog. (2019). Retrieved from https://www.precision-dog-training.com/

Phenix, A. 5 Training Tips for Your Working Dog Breed. (2017). Retrieved from https://www.dogster.com/dog-training/training-tips-for-your-working-dog-breed

Phenix, A. How to Prep for the First Two Months of Puppy Training. (2019). Retrieved from https://www.dogster.com/puppies/first-two-months-puppy-training-prep

Re-Housetraining Your Adult Dog. (2019). Retrieved from https://www.paws.org/library/dogs/training/re-housetraining/

Rollins, J. How to Discipline a Puppy or Dog: Effectively Punishing Your Dog. (2016). Retrieved from https://www.petexpertise.com/dog-training-article-using-physical-punishments/

Secrets To Housebreaking Adult Dogs. (2019). Retrieved from https://www.cesarsway.com/secrets-to-housebreaking-adult-dogs/

Shea, T. How to Train a Puppy: The First 8 Things You Need to Do. (2019). Retrieved from https://www.rd.com/advice/pets/how-to-train-your-puppy/

Stregowski, J. How to Solve 10 of the Biggest Dog Behavior Problems. (2019). Retrieved from https://www.thesprucepets.com/common-dog-behavior-problems-1118278

Stregowski, J. This Step by Step Guide Can Help You Completely Train Your Dog. (2019). Retrieved from https://www.thesprucepets.com/steps-to-train-your-dog-1118273

Teaching old dogs new tricks. (2019). Retrieved from https://dogtime.com/lifestyle/dog-activities/1161-training-adult-senior-dogs-aaha

The Basics of Puppy Training. (2019). Retrieved from https://www.zooplus.co.uk/magazine/dog/dog-training/basics-puppy-training

The Do's And Don'ts Of Positive Reinforcement. (2019). Retrieved from https://www.cesarsway.com/the-dos-and-donts-of-positive-reinforcement/

The Importance of Training Your Dog. (2019). Retrieved from https://www.greenacreskennel.com/dog-behavior-and-training/the-importance-of-training-your-dog.html

Theis, T., & Conway, K. Top Ten Dog Training Tips. (2019). Retrieved from https://www.petfinder.com/dogs/dog-training/dog-training-tips/

Tips for Solving Common Behavior Problems. (2019). Retrieved from https://www.nylabone.com/dog101/tips-for-solving-common-behavior-problems

Top 5 Best Dog Training Super Tips For Beginners. (2019). Retrieved from https://sitstay.com/blogs/good-dog-blog/95094215-top-5-best-dog-training-super-tips-for-beginners

Top 10 Hardest Dog Breeds to Train. (2017). Retrieved from https://canna-pet.com/top-10-hardest-dog-breeds-train/

Training An Older Dog - You Can Teach An Old Dog New Tricks!. (2019). Retrieved from https://www.fidosavvy.com/training-an-older-dog.html

Training Older Dogs - Tips & Advice That Work. (2019). Retrieved from https://www.seniortailwaggers.com/training-older-dogs/

Treat training for dogs. (2019). Retrieved from https://www.cesarsway.com/tricks-for-treats-training-your-dog-with-food/

Vuckovic, A. How to Discipline a Dog Without Hitting, Advice and Tips. (2017). Retrieved from https://petcube.com/blog/dog-training/

Waggener, N. Five Basic Obedience Commands Your Dog Should Learn. (2018). Retrieved from https://www.southbostonanimalhospital.com/blog/five-basic-obedience-commands-your-dog-should-learn

Welton, M. Puppy Training Schedule: What to Teach Puppies, and When. (2019). Retrieved from https://www.yourpurebredpuppy.com/training/articles/puppy-training-schedule.html

White, P. MASTERCLASSES; DOG TRAINING; How to teach young dogs new tricks. (1995). Retrieved from https://www.independent.co.uk/arts-entertainment/masterclasses-dog-training-how-to-teach-young-dogs-new-tricks-1526258.html

Wondra, S. Large Dog Training Tips. (2019). Retrieved from https://www.petcarerx.com/article/large-dog-training-tips/862

Woods, J. Puppy Training Tips: 45 Dog Experts Share Their Secrets. (2018). Retrieved from https://www.allthingsdogs.com/puppy-training-tips/

Wright, M. Philosophy. (2019). Retrieved from https://www.argostraining.com/positive-dog-training-philosophy/

www.ingramcontent.com/pod-product-compliance
Lightning Source LLC
Chambersburg PA
CBHW072016110526
44592CB00012B/1323